MATH

Grade 2

Thomas J. Richards
Mathematics Teacher
Lamar Junior-Senior High School
Lamar, Missouri

Marjorie Diggs Freeman
Basic Skills Enrichment Program
Shark River Hills School
Neptune, New Jersey

Grand Rapids, Michigan

Frank Schaffer Publications®

Printed in the United States of America. All rights reserved. Limited Reproduction Permission: Permission to duplicate these materials is limited to the person for whom they are purchased. Reproduction for an entire school or school district is unlawful and strictly prohibited. Frank Schaffer Publications is an imprint of School Specialty Publishing. Copyright © 2003 School Specialty Publishing.

Send all inquiries to:
Frank Schaffer Publications
3195 Wilson Drive NW
Grand Rapids, MI 49534

ISBN 1-56189-902-X

9 10 11 12 13 VHG 09 08 07 06 05

Table of Contents

SPECTRUM MATHEMATICS

For each chapter there is a PRE-TEST, instructional material, written exercises, verbal problems, and a CHECKUP. There is also a 2-page CHECKUP covering the first half of the book, and a 4-page FINAL CHECKUP covering the entire book.

Record of Checkup Scores

Rank	Test Pages								
	9	19	35	51	71	89	109–10	111–2	113–6

(Chart of vertical scales with ranks: Excellent, Very Good, Good, Fair, Poor)

	9	19	35	51	71	89	109–10	111–2	113–6
Excellent	36, 35	36, 35	26, 25	10, 9	26, 25	22, 20	30	50	70
Very Good	30, 25	30, 25	20	8, 7	20	15	25, 20	40	60, 50
Good	20	20	15	6, 5	15		15	30	40
Fair	15	15	10	4, 3	10	10	10	20	30
Poor	10, 5, 0	10, 5, 0	5, 0	2, 1, 0	5, 0	5, 0	5, 0	10, 0	20, 10, 0

To record the score you receive on each CHECKUP:

(1) Find the vertical scale below the page number of that CHECKUP,
(2) on that vertical scale, draw a ● at the mark which represents your score.

For example, if you score the CHECKUP on page 9 as "My score: 25," draw a ● at the 25-mark on the first vertical scale. A score of 25 would show that your rank is "Good." You can check your progress from one checkup to the next by connecting the dots with a line segment.

Lesson 1 Numbers 0 Through 10

NAME _____

Write the numeral for each number.

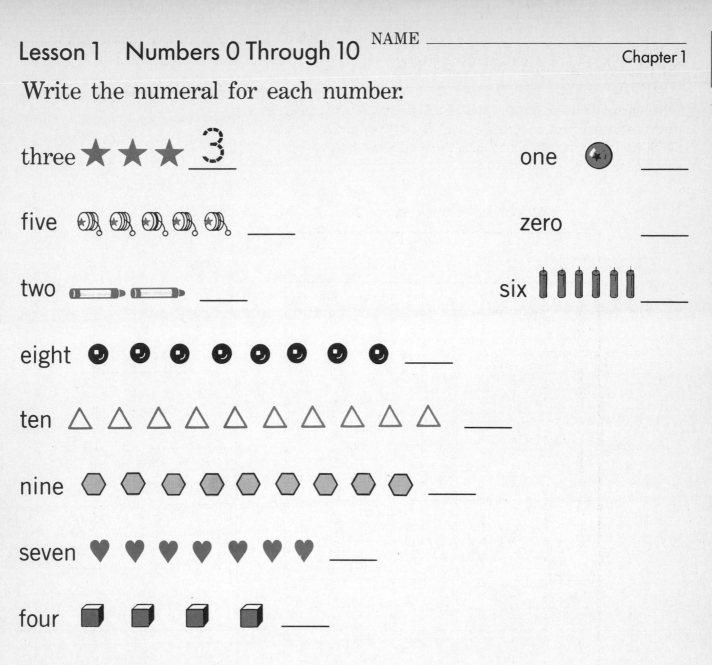

three ★ ★ ★ _3_   one _____

five _____   zero _____

two _____   six _____

eight _____

ten _____

nine _____

seven _____

four _____

Tell how many dots.

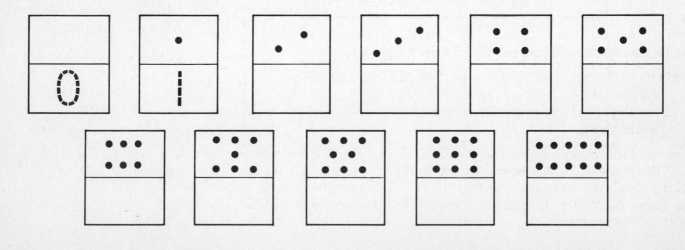

Lesson 2   Facts Through 5

Add or subtract.

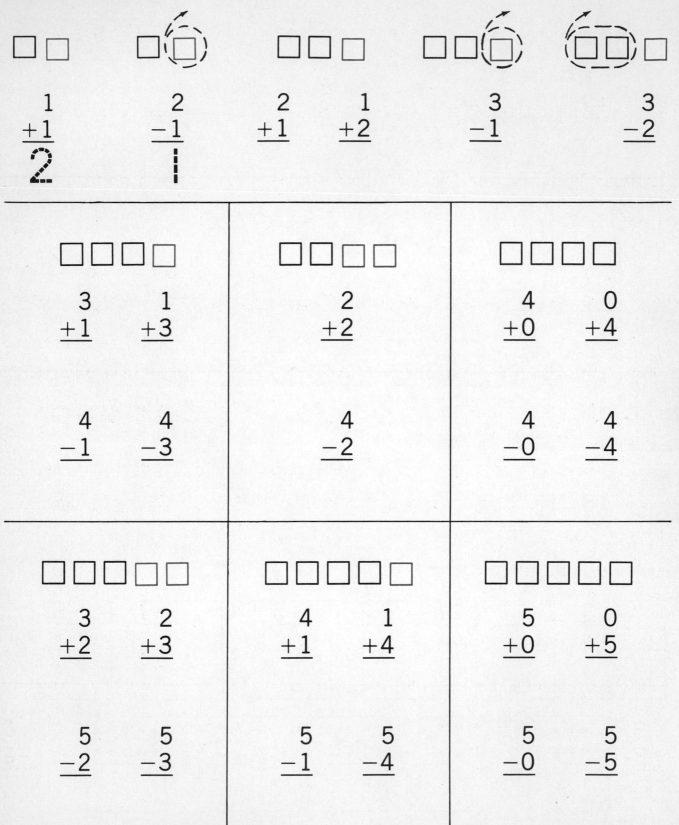

1 +1 **2**	2 −1 I	2 +1	1 +2	3 −1	3 −2

3 +1	1 +3	2 +2	4 +0	0 +4
4 −1	4 −3	4 −2	4 −0	4 −4

3 +2	2 +3	4 +1	1 +4	5 +0	0 +5
5 −2	5 −3	5 −1	5 −4	5 −0	5 −5

Perfect score: 28   My score: _____

Lesson 3   Facts for 6 and 7

Add or subtract.

$$\begin{array}{cc} 5 \\ +1 \\ \hline 6 \end{array} \quad \begin{array}{c} 1 \\ +5 \end{array} \qquad \begin{array}{c} 6 \\ -1 \\ \hline 5 \end{array} \qquad \begin{array}{c} 6 \\ -5 \end{array}$$

$$\begin{array}{cc} 3 & 6 \\ +3 & -3 \end{array} \qquad \begin{array}{cccc} 4 & 2 & 6 & 6 \\ +2 & +4 & -2 & -4 \end{array}$$

$$\begin{array}{cc} 4 & 3 \\ +3 & +4 \end{array} \qquad \begin{array}{cc} 5 & 2 \\ +2 & +5 \end{array} \qquad \begin{array}{cc} 6 & 1 \\ +1 & +6 \end{array}$$

$$\begin{array}{cc} 7 & 7 \\ -3 & -4 \end{array} \qquad \begin{array}{cc} 7 & 7 \\ -2 & -5 \end{array} \qquad \begin{array}{cc} 7 & 7 \\ -1 & -6 \end{array}$$

$$\begin{array}{ccc} 3 & 5 & 6 \\ +3 & +2 & +0 \end{array} \qquad \begin{array}{ccc} 7 & 7 & 6 \\ -7 & -4 & -2 \end{array}$$

Perfect score: 28   My score: _____

3

Lesson 4   Facts for 8
Add or subtract.

```
  5      3              8                    8
 +3     +5             -3                   -5
 ‗8‗                  ‗5‗
```

```
    4              6      2              7      1
   +4             +2     +6             +1     +7


    8              8      8              8      8
   -4             -2     -6             -1     -7
```

```
  2      4      5      3      7      0
 +6     +3     +1     +5     +1     +8


  8      7      8      6      8      8
 -1     -6     -5     -3     -0     -2
```

Lesson 5   Facts for 9

Add or subtract.

$$\begin{array}{r} 5 \\ +4 \\ \hline 9 \end{array} \qquad \begin{array}{r} 4 \\ +5 \\ \hline \end{array} \qquad\qquad \begin{array}{r} 9 \\ -4 \\ \hline 5 \end{array} \qquad\qquad \begin{array}{r} 9 \\ -5 \\ \hline \end{array}$$

$$\begin{array}{r} 6 \\ +3 \\ \hline \end{array} \qquad \begin{array}{r} 3 \\ +6 \\ \hline \end{array} \qquad \begin{array}{r} 7 \\ +2 \\ \hline \end{array} \qquad \begin{array}{r} 2 \\ +7 \\ \hline \end{array} \qquad \begin{array}{r} 8 \\ +1 \\ \hline \end{array} \qquad \begin{array}{r} 1 \\ +8 \\ \hline \end{array}$$

$$\begin{array}{r} 9 \\ -3 \\ \hline \end{array} \qquad \begin{array}{r} 9 \\ -6 \\ \hline \end{array} \qquad \begin{array}{r} 9 \\ -2 \\ \hline \end{array} \qquad \begin{array}{r} 9 \\ -7 \\ \hline \end{array} \qquad \begin{array}{r} 9 \\ -1 \\ \hline \end{array} \qquad \begin{array}{r} 9 \\ -8 \\ \hline \end{array}$$

$$\begin{array}{r} 5 \\ +4 \\ \hline \end{array} \qquad \begin{array}{r} 2 \\ +7 \\ \hline \end{array} \qquad \begin{array}{r} 6 \\ +1 \\ \hline \end{array} \qquad \begin{array}{r} 9 \\ +0 \\ \hline \end{array} \qquad \begin{array}{r} 1 \\ +8 \\ \hline \end{array} \qquad \begin{array}{r} 4 \\ +4 \\ \hline \end{array}$$

$$\begin{array}{r} 9 \\ -5 \\ \hline \end{array} \qquad \begin{array}{r} 7 \\ -3 \\ \hline \end{array} \qquad \begin{array}{r} 9 \\ -8 \\ \hline \end{array} \qquad \begin{array}{r} 9 \\ -3 \\ \hline \end{array} \qquad \begin{array}{r} 9 \\ -9 \\ \hline \end{array} \qquad \begin{array}{r} 9 \\ -0 \\ \hline \end{array}$$

Perfect score: 28   My score: _____

5

Lesson 6   Facts for 10

Add or subtract.

5	6 4
+5	+4 +6
10	
10	10 10
− 5	− 4 − 6
5	

7   3
+3   +7

10   10
− 3   − 7

8   2
+2   +8

10   10
− 2   − 8

9   1
+1   +9

10   10
− 1   − 9

4   5   9   10   10   10
+6   +5   +1   − 8   − 3   − 0

Lesson 7 Facts Through 10
Add.

5 +4 9	4 +3	1 +2	5 +3	4 +6	4 +4
0 +6	4 +1	8 +1	9 +1	8 +2	2 +2
2 +7	5 +2	1 +6	5 +5	4 +5	6 +2

Subtract.

10 − 6 4	8 −2	5 −3	7 −6	4 −3	10 − 5
9 −3	10 − 2	7 −2	8 −6	10 − 9	8 −8
10 − 4	9 −6	9 −8	8 −1	10 − 7	7 −4

Perfect score: 36   My score: _____

Problem Solving

Solve each problem.

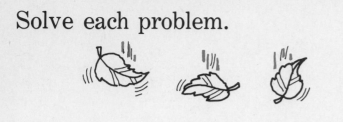

$$\begin{array}{r} 4 \\ + 3 \\ \hline 7 \end{array}$$

leaves on the ground
leaves falling
leaves in all

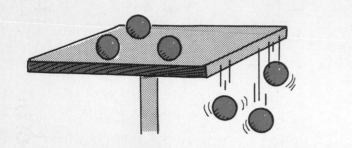

_____ balls in all
−_____ balls falling
_____ balls not falling

_____ fish by a rock
+_____ more fish coming
_____ fish in all

_____ pencils in all
−_____ pencils taken
_____ pencils not taken

_____ puppies on a rug
+_____ more puppies coming
_____ puppies in all

Perfect score: 5   My score: _____

8

Chapter 1   Checkup

Add.

2	7	4	6	2	0
+4	+3	+5	+2	+3	+4

4	1	2	3	6	2
+3	+5	+8	+3	+4	+1

3	7	8	5	3	5
+1	+0	+1	+2	+6	+5

Subtract.

3	5	10	9	7	10
−3	−2	− 6	−2	−3	− 5

9	8	1	6	8	10
−1	−7	−0	−4	−5	− 8

9	4	6	7	10	8
−6	−3	−3	−5	− 9	−4

Perfect score: 36   My score: _____

PRE-TEST

2

Tell how many.

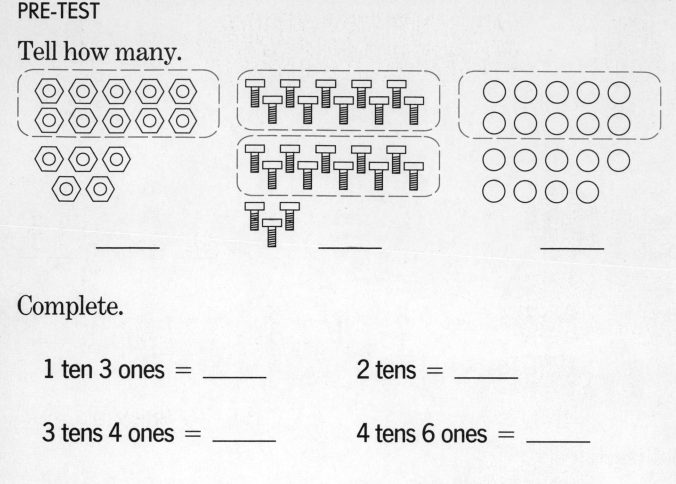

_____   _____   _____

Complete.

1 ten 3 ones = _____   2 tens = _____

3 tens 4 ones = _____   4 tens 6 ones = _____

8 tens = _____   7 tens 9 ones = _____

Name the next four numbers.

6, 7, 8, _____, _____, _____, _____

24, 25, 26, _____, _____, _____, _____

50, 51, 52, _____, _____, _____, _____

67, 68, 69, _____, _____, _____, _____

Perfect score: 25   My score: _____

Lesson 1 Numbers 11 Through 18

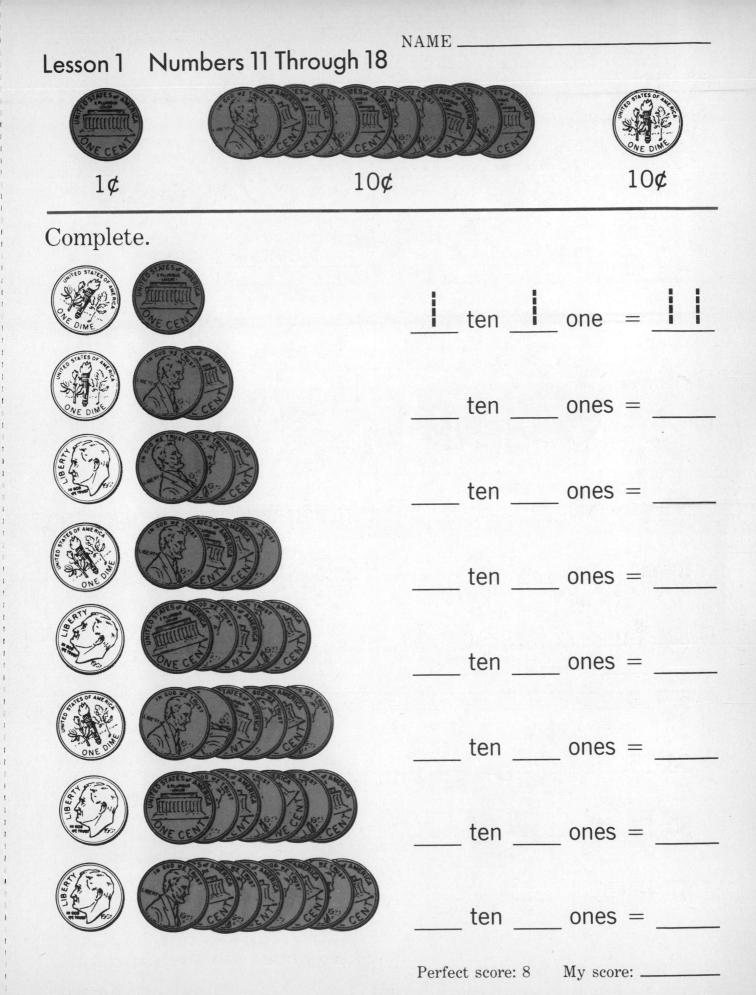

1¢   10¢   10¢

Complete.

___ ten ___ one = _____

___ ten ___ ones = _____

___ ten ___ ones = _____

___ ten ___ ones = _____

___ ten ___ ones = _____

___ ten ___ ones = _____

___ ten ___ ones = _____

___ ten ___ ones = _____

Perfect score: 8   My score: _____

Lesson 2   Numbers 19 Through 39
Complete.

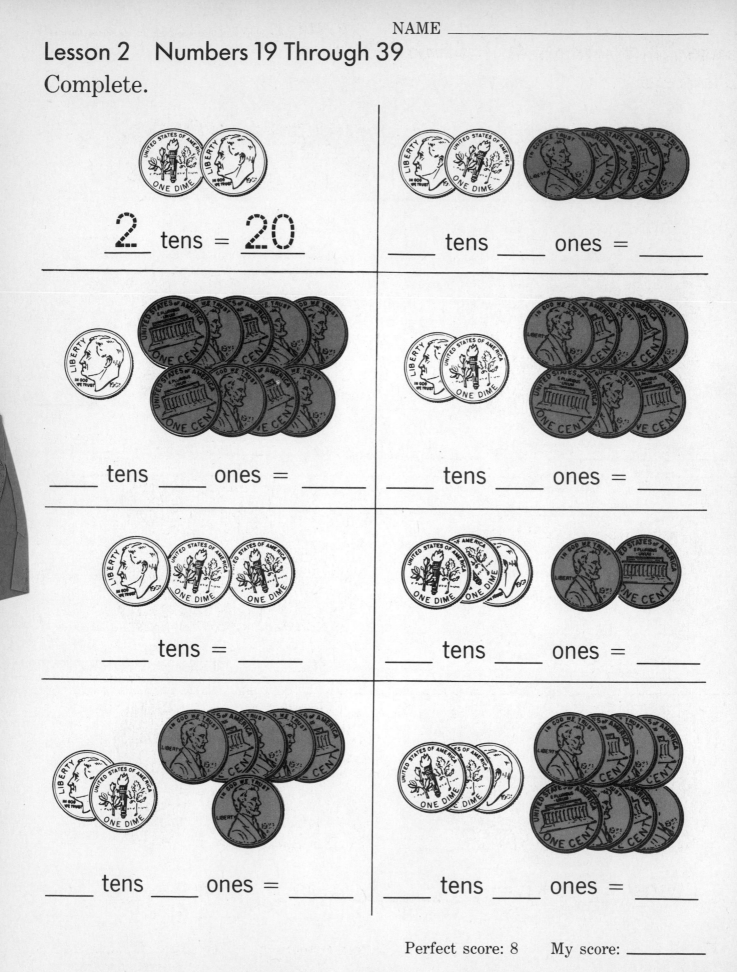

__2__ tens = __20__

___ tens ___ ones = ___

___ tens ___ ones = ___

___ tens ___ ones = ___

___ tens = ___

___ tens ___ ones = ___

___ tens ___ ones = ___

___ tens ___ ones = ___

Perfect score: 8   My score: _____

Lesson 3   Numbers 40 Through 99
Complete.

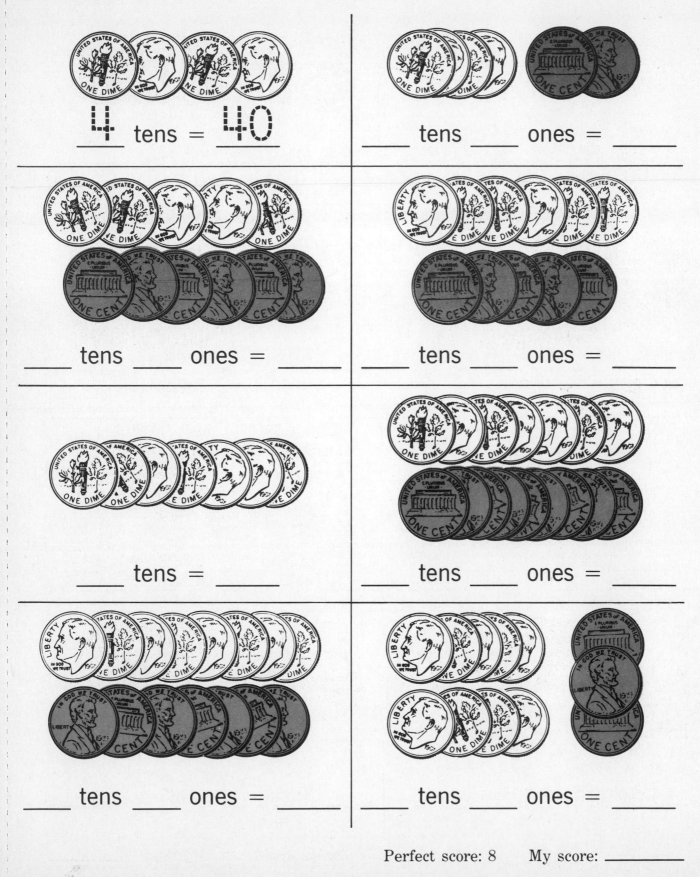

____4____ tens = 40

_____ tens _____ ones = _____

_____ tens _____ ones = _____

_____ tens _____ ones = _____

_____ tens = _____

_____ tens _____ ones = _____

_____ tens _____ ones = _____

_____ tens _____ ones = _____

Perfect score: 8   My score: _____

13

Complete.

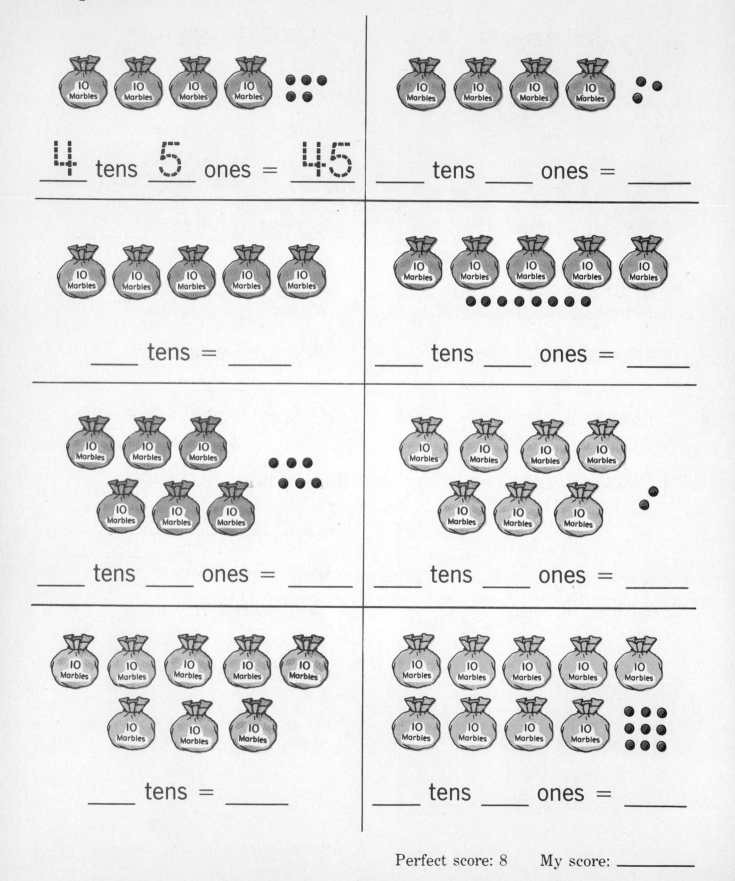

___ tens ___ ones = ___

___ tens ___ ones = ___

___ tens = ___

___ tens ___ ones = ___

___ tens ___ ones = ___

___ tens ___ ones = ___

___ tens = ___

___ tens ___ ones = ___

Perfect score: 8   My score: _____

14

Lesson 4   Numbers Through 99
Complete.

4 tens 6 ones = **46**   2 tens 1 one = _____

1 ten 2 ones = _____   5 tens 7 ones = _____

3 tens 7 ones = _____   1 ten 9 ones = _____

2 tens 4 ones = _____   8 tens 8 ones = _____

9 tens = _____   6 tens 7 ones = _____

6 tens = _____   7 tens 2 ones = _____

5 tens 3 ones = _____   9 tens 5 ones = _____

7 tens 8 ones = _____   4 tens 1 one = _____

1 ten 1 one = _____   3 tens 4 ones = _____

8 tens 4 ones = _____   6 tens 6 ones = _____

3 tens 5 ones = _____   8 tens 9 ones = _____

4 tens 9 ones = _____   2 tens = _____

9 tens 6 ones = _____   5 tens = _____

Numbers Through 99

Name numbers in order.

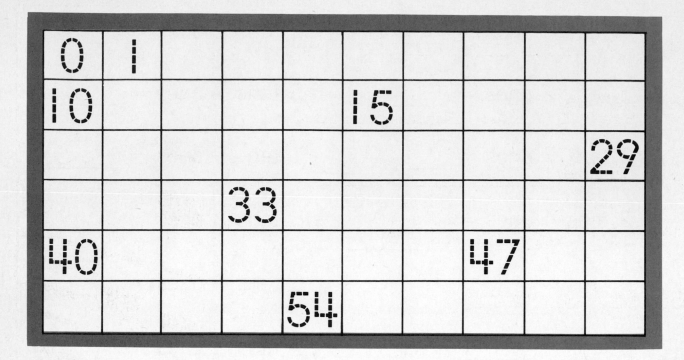

0	1								
10				15					
									29
			33						
40							47		
				54					

Connect the dots in order.

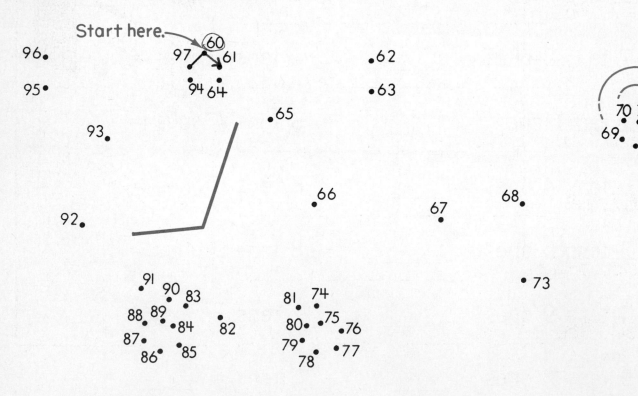

Start here.

60
96•   97 61
95•   94 64   •62
93•   •63
92•   •65
           •66   67   68•
                      • 73
91
90 83
88 89 81 74
87• •84 82 80• •75 76
86• •85 79• •77
78

69• 70 71
•72

Name the next four numbers.

6, 7, 8, __9__ , __10__ , __11__ , __12__

22, 23, 24, _____, _____, _____, _____

37, 38, 39, _____, _____, _____, _____

15, 16, 17, _____, _____, _____, _____

51, 52, 53, _____, _____, _____, _____

44, 45, 46, _____, _____, _____, _____

76, 77, 78, _____, _____, _____, _____

82, 83, 84, _____, _____, _____, _____

68, 69, 70, _____, _____, _____, _____

86, 87, 88, _____, _____, _____, _____

55, 56, 57, _____, _____, _____, _____

93, 94, 95, _____, _____, _____, _____

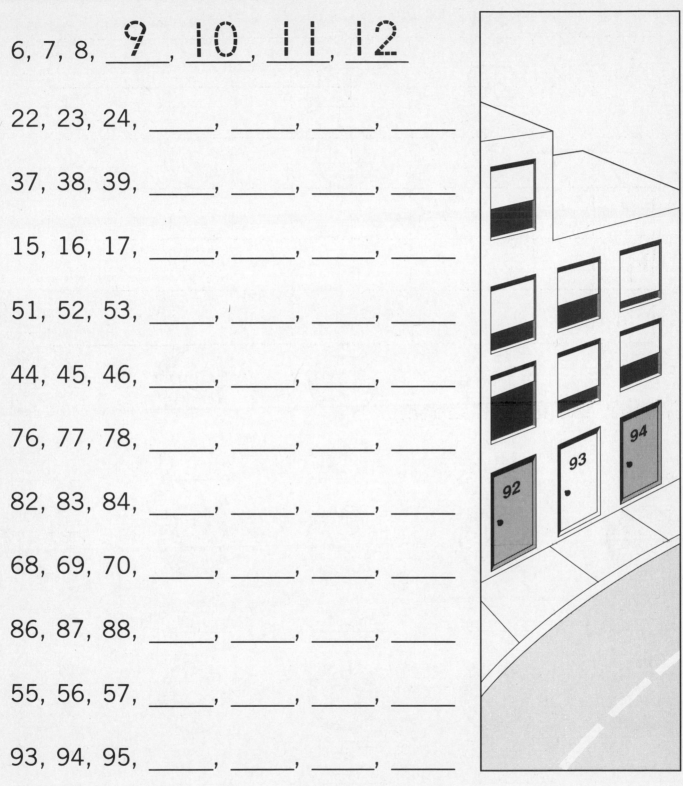

Perfect score: 48   My score: _____

17

Lesson 6   Skip Counting

Count by 10.

10, 20, 30, ____, ____,

____, ____, ____, ____

Count by 5.

5, 10, 15, ____, ____,

____, ____, ____, ____, ____,

____, ____, ____, ____, ____

Perfect score: 24   My score: _____

18

NAME _____

Complete.

2 tens 8 ones = _____   5 tens = _____

3 tens 1 one = _____   4 tens 5 ones = _____

7 tens = _____   8 tens 2 ones = _____

6 tens 6 ones = _____   9 tens 8 ones = _____

9 tens = _____   7 tens 9 ones = _____

Name the next four numbers.

4, 5, 6, _____, _____, _____, _____

37, 38, 39, _____, _____, _____, _____

53, 54, 55, _____, _____, _____, _____

61, 62, 63, _____, _____, _____, _____

78, 79, 80, _____, _____, _____, _____

86, 87, 88, _____, _____, _____, _____

Perfect score: 34   My score: _____

PRE-TEST

Add.

3 +4	5 +4	2 +8	7 +2	4 +6	6 +2
5 +7	3 +8	9 +4	6 +6	8 +5	2 +9
7 +7	9 +6	8 +7	4 +9	8 +8	6 +8

Subtract.

6 −3	5 −4	9 −7	8 −2	1 0 − 7	7 −0
1 1 − 7	1 3 − 6	1 1 − 5	1 2 − 4	1 3 − 4	1 2 − 9
1 4 − 5	1 7 − 9	1 6 − 7	1 4 − 7	1 5 − 6	1 8 − 9

Perfect score: 36   My score: _____

NAME _____

Add.

$$\begin{array}{r} 2 \\ +9 \\ \hline 11 \end{array}$$
　✲　✲✲✲
　✲　✲✲✲
　　✲✲✲
$$\begin{array}{r} 9 \\ +2 \\ \hline \end{array}$$
$$\begin{array}{r} 3 \\ +8 \\ \hline \end{array}$$
　✲　✲✲✲
　✲　✲✲
　✲　✲✲✲
$$\begin{array}{r} 8 \\ +3 \\ \hline \end{array}$$

$$\begin{array}{r} 6 \\ +5 \\ \hline \end{array}$$
　✲✲　✲✲
　　✲　✲✲
　✲✲　✲✲
$$\begin{array}{r} 5 \\ +6 \\ \hline \end{array}$$
$$\begin{array}{r} 4 \\ +7 \\ \hline \end{array}$$
　✲✲　✲✲
　✲✲　✲✲✲
　　　　✲✲
$$\begin{array}{r} 7 \\ +4 \\ \hline \end{array}$$

$$\begin{array}{r} 8 \\ +4 \\ \hline \end{array}$$
　✲✲　✲✲
　✲✲　✲✲
　✲✲
　✲✲
$$\begin{array}{r} 4 \\ +8 \\ \hline \end{array}$$
$$\begin{array}{r} 7 \\ +5 \\ \hline \end{array}$$
　✲✲　✲✲
　✲✲　　✲
　✲✲　✲✲
　✲
$$\begin{array}{r} 5 \\ +7 \\ \hline \end{array}$$

$$\begin{array}{r} 9 \\ +3 \\ \hline \end{array}$$
　✲✲✲　✲
　✲✲✲　✲✲
　✲✲✲　✲
$$\begin{array}{r} 3 \\ +9 \\ \hline \end{array}$$
$$\begin{array}{r} 6 \\ +6 \\ \hline \end{array}$$
　✲✲✲　✲✲✲
　✲✲✲　✲✲✲

Add.

$$\begin{array}{r} 8 \\ +3 \\ \hline \end{array} \qquad \begin{array}{r} 6 \\ +6 \\ \hline \end{array} \qquad \begin{array}{r} 9 \\ +3 \\ \hline \end{array} \qquad \begin{array}{r} 3 \\ +8 \\ \hline \end{array} \qquad \begin{array}{r} 4 \\ +7 \\ \hline \end{array} \qquad \begin{array}{r} 2 \\ +9 \\ \hline \end{array}$$

$$\begin{array}{r} 5 \\ +7 \\ \hline \end{array} \qquad \begin{array}{r} 8 \\ +4 \\ \hline \end{array} \qquad \begin{array}{r} 7 \\ +5 \\ \hline \end{array} \qquad \begin{array}{r} 5 \\ +6 \\ \hline \end{array} \qquad \begin{array}{r} 9 \\ +2 \\ \hline \end{array} \qquad \begin{array}{r} 4 \\ +8 \\ \hline \end{array}$$

Perfect score: 27   My score: _____

Problem Solving

Solve each problem.

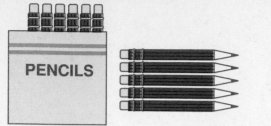 pencils in a box

more pencils

pencils in all

 grapes on a plate

more grapes

grapes in all

 marbles in one hand

marbles in the other hand

marbles in all

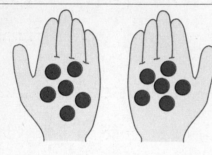 people at the table

more people coming in

people in all

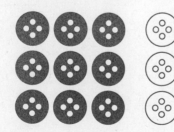 black buttons

white buttons

buttons in all

Lesson 2   Subtraction Facts Through 12

Subtract.

11 − 9		11 − 2	11 − 8		11 − 3	
11 − 6		11 − 5	11 − 7		11 −4	
12 − 8		12 − 4	12 − 7		12 − 5	
12 − 9		12 − 3	12 − 6			

Subtract.

11	11	12	11	12	12
− 3	− 6	− 3	− 8	− 7	− 9

11	12	12	12	11	12
− 7	− 4	− 5	− 6	− 2	− 8

Problem Solving

Solve each problem.

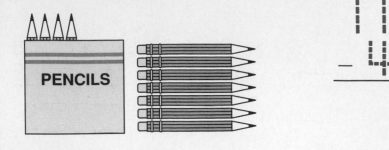

	pencils in all
1 1	
− 4	pencils in the box
	pencils not in the box

people in all

people are leaving

people are staying

oranges in all

oranges in the bowl

oranges not in the bowl

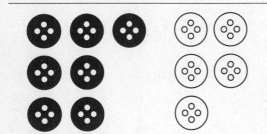

buttons in all

black buttons

white buttons

candles in all

candles lit

candles not lit

Perfect score: 5   My score: _____

24

NAME _____

Add.

$$\begin{array}{r} 6 \\ +7 \\ \hline 13 \end{array}$$

$$\begin{array}{r} 7 \\ +6 \\ \hline \end{array}$$

$$\begin{array}{r} 5 \\ +8 \\ \hline \end{array}$$

$$\begin{array}{r} 8 \\ +5 \\ \hline \end{array}$$

$$\begin{array}{r} 9 \\ +4 \\ \hline \end{array}$$

$$\begin{array}{r} 4 \\ +9 \\ \hline \end{array}$$

$$\begin{array}{r} 9 \\ +5 \\ \hline \end{array}$$

$$\begin{array}{r} 5 \\ +9 \\ \hline \end{array}$$

$$\begin{array}{r} 8 \\ +6 \\ \hline \end{array}$$

$$\begin{array}{r} 6 \\ +8 \\ \hline \end{array}$$

$$\begin{array}{r} 7 \\ +7 \\ \hline \end{array}$$

Add.

$$\begin{array}{r} 7 \\ +7 \\ \hline \end{array} \qquad \begin{array}{r} 5 \\ +8 \\ \hline \end{array} \qquad \begin{array}{r} 9 \\ +4 \\ \hline \end{array} \qquad \begin{array}{r} 8 \\ +6 \\ \hline \end{array} \qquad \begin{array}{r} 4 \\ +9 \\ \hline \end{array} \qquad \begin{array}{r} 5 \\ +9 \\ \hline \end{array}$$

$$\begin{array}{r} 8 \\ +5 \\ \hline \end{array} \qquad \begin{array}{r} 6 \\ +8 \\ \hline \end{array} \qquad \begin{array}{r} 9 \\ +5 \\ \hline \end{array} \qquad \begin{array}{r} 6 \\ +6 \\ \hline \end{array} \qquad \begin{array}{r} 7 \\ +6 \\ \hline \end{array} \qquad \begin{array}{r} 6 \\ +7 \\ \hline \end{array}$$

Perfect score: 23   My score: _____

25

NAME _____

Lesson 4   Subtraction Facts Through 14

Subtract.

$$\begin{array}{r}1\ 3\\-\ 5\\\hline 8\end{array}\qquad\begin{array}{r}1\ 4\\-\ 9\\\hline 5\end{array}$$

$$\begin{array}{r}1\ 4\\-\ 8\\\hline\end{array}\qquad\begin{array}{r}1\ 3\\-\ 4\\\hline\end{array}$$

$$\begin{array}{r}1\ 3\\-\ 6\\\hline\end{array}\qquad\begin{array}{r}1\ 4\\-\ 5\\\hline\end{array}$$

Subtract.

$$\begin{array}{r}1\ 2\\-\ 7\\\hline 5\end{array}\quad\begin{array}{r}1\ 0\\-\ 2\\\hline\end{array}\quad\begin{array}{r}1\ 3\\-\ 4\\\hline\end{array}\quad\begin{array}{r}1\ 4\\-\ 9\\\hline\end{array}\quad\begin{array}{r}1\ 1\\-\ 8\\\hline\end{array}\quad\begin{array}{r}1\ 4\\-\ 5\\\hline\end{array}$$

$$\begin{array}{r}1\ 4\\-\ 6\\\hline\end{array}\quad\begin{array}{r}1\ 2\\-\ 8\\\hline\end{array}\quad\begin{array}{r}1\ 3\\-\ 5\\\hline\end{array}\quad\begin{array}{r}1\ 0\\-\ 6\\\hline\end{array}\quad\begin{array}{r}1\ 3\\-\ 6\\\hline\end{array}\quad\begin{array}{r}1\ 3\\-\ 7\\\hline\end{array}$$

$$\begin{array}{r}1\ 1\\-\ 6\\\hline\end{array}\quad\begin{array}{r}1\ 3\\-\ 9\\\hline\end{array}\quad\begin{array}{r}1\ 4\\-\ 8\\\hline\end{array}\quad\begin{array}{r}1\ 2\\-\ 3\\\hline\end{array}\quad\begin{array}{r}1\ 4\\-\ 7\\\hline\end{array}\quad\begin{array}{r}1\ 3\\-\ 8\\\hline\end{array}$$

Perfect score: 24   My score: _____

26

NAME _____

Add.

$$\begin{array}{r} 6 \\ +9 \\ \hline 15 \end{array}$$

$$\begin{array}{r} 9 \\ +6 \\ \hline \end{array}$$

$$\begin{array}{r} 8 \\ +7 \\ \hline \end{array}$$

$$\begin{array}{r} 7 \\ +8 \\ \hline \end{array}$$

$$\begin{array}{r} 9 \\ +7 \\ \hline \end{array}$$

$$\begin{array}{r} 7 \\ +9 \\ \hline \end{array}$$

$$\begin{array}{r} 8 \\ +9 \\ \hline \end{array}$$

$$\begin{array}{r} 9 \\ +8 \\ \hline \end{array}$$

$$\begin{array}{r} 8 \\ +8 \\ \hline \end{array}$$

$$\begin{array}{r} 9 \\ +9 \\ \hline \end{array}$$

Add.

$$\begin{array}{r} 9 \\ +6 \\ \hline 15 \end{array}$$

$$\begin{array}{r} 7 \\ +8 \\ \hline \end{array}$$

$$\begin{array}{r} 9 \\ +9 \\ \hline \end{array}$$

$$\begin{array}{r} 7 \\ +9 \\ \hline \end{array}$$

$$\begin{array}{r} 8 \\ +9 \\ \hline \end{array}$$

$$\begin{array}{r} 6 \\ +9 \\ \hline \end{array}$$

$$\begin{array}{r} 9 \\ +8 \\ \hline \end{array}$$

$$\begin{array}{r} 8 \\ +8 \\ \hline \end{array}$$

$$\begin{array}{r} 9 \\ +7 \\ \hline \end{array}$$

$$\begin{array}{r} 8 \\ +7 \\ \hline \end{array}$$

$$\begin{array}{r} 9 \\ +5 \\ \hline \end{array}$$

$$\begin{array}{r} 7 \\ +7 \\ \hline \end{array}$$

$$\begin{array}{r} 9 \\ +3 \\ \hline \end{array}$$

$$\begin{array}{r} 8 \\ +5 \\ \hline \end{array}$$

$$\begin{array}{r} 7 \\ +6 \\ \hline \end{array}$$

$$\begin{array}{r} 8 \\ +6 \\ \hline \end{array}$$

$$\begin{array}{r} 9 \\ +4 \\ \hline \end{array}$$

$$\begin{array}{r} 7 \\ +5 \\ \hline \end{array}$$

Perfect score: 28   My score: _____

Problem Solving

Solve each problem.

	_9_ black sheep
	_+ 9_ white sheep
	sheep in all

_____ softballs

_____ baseballs

_____ softballs and baseballs

_____ glasses of milk

_____ empty glasses

_____ glasses in all

_____ white socks

_____ gray socks

_____ socks in all

_____ bow ties

_____ regular ties

_____ ties in all

Lesson 6 Subtraction Facts Through 18

Subtract.

	$\begin{array}{r} 1\ 5 \\ -\ 7 \\ \hline 8 \end{array}$		$\begin{array}{r} 1\ 6 \\ -\ 9 \\ \hline \end{array}$
	$\begin{array}{r} 1\ 7 \\ -\ 8 \\ \hline \end{array}$		$\begin{array}{r} 1\ 8 \\ -\ 9 \\ \hline \end{array}$

Subtract.

$\begin{array}{r} 1\ 8 \\ -9 \\ \hline 9 \end{array}$	$\begin{array}{r} 1\ 3 \\ -\ 5 \\ \hline \end{array}$	$\begin{array}{r} 1\ 6 \\ -\ 8 \\ \hline \end{array}$	$\begin{array}{r} 1\ 7 \\ -\ 9 \\ \hline \end{array}$	$\begin{array}{r} 1\ 4 \\ -\ 6 \\ \hline \end{array}$	$\begin{array}{r} 1\ 3 \\ -\ 9 \\ \hline \end{array}$
$\begin{array}{r} 1\ 7 \\ -\ 8 \\ \hline \end{array}$	$\begin{array}{r} 1\ 5 \\ -\ 9 \\ \hline \end{array}$	$\begin{array}{r} 1\ 4 \\ -\ 5 \\ \hline \end{array}$	$\begin{array}{r} 1\ 3 \\ -\ 6 \\ \hline \end{array}$	$\begin{array}{r} 1\ 6 \\ -\ 7 \\ \hline \end{array}$	$\begin{array}{r} 1\ 2 \\ -\ 4 \\ \hline \end{array}$
$\begin{array}{r} 1\ 4 \\ -\ 7 \\ \hline \end{array}$	$\begin{array}{r} 1\ 5 \\ -\ 8 \\ \hline \end{array}$	$\begin{array}{r} 1\ 6 \\ -\ 9 \\ \hline \end{array}$	$\begin{array}{r} 1\ 2 \\ -\ 7 \\ \hline \end{array}$	$\begin{array}{r} 1\ 5 \\ -\ 7 \\ \hline \end{array}$	$\begin{array}{r} 1\ 3 \\ -\ 4 \\ \hline \end{array}$
$\begin{array}{r} 1\ 5 \\ -\ 6 \\ \hline \end{array}$	$\begin{array}{r} 1\ 4 \\ -\ 8 \\ \hline \end{array}$	$\begin{array}{r} 1\ 2 \\ -\ 3 \\ \hline \end{array}$	$\begin{array}{r} 1\ 3 \\ -\ 9 \\ \hline \end{array}$	$\begin{array}{r} 1\ 4 \\ -\ 9 \\ \hline \end{array}$	$\begin{array}{r} 1\ 1 \\ -\ 3 \\ \hline \end{array}$

Perfect score: 28   My score: _____

Problem Solving

Solve each problem.

There are 12 dogs.

3 run away.

How many dogs are left?

$$\begin{array}{r} 12 \\ -\ 3 \\ \hline 9 \end{array}$$

Roger has 10 marbles.

Roger loses 3 marbles.

How many marbles are left?

Mary has 16 black shoes.

Mike has 8 black shoes.

How many more shoes does Mary
have than Mike?

There are 14 cows in the field.

9 cows come to the barn.

How many cows are left in the field?

There are 18 horses running.

There are 9 horses standing.

How many more horses are running
than standing?

Perfect score: 5   My score: _____

Lesson 7   Mixed Practice Facts Through 18

Add.

9	5	7	4	9	7
$+7$	$+9$	$+8$	$+9$	$+9$	$+7$
16					

6	8	9	7	8	7
$+9$	$+6$	$+5$	$+9$	$+9$	$+6$

8	6	9	8	9	8
$+8$	$+8$	$+6$	$+5$	$+8$	$+7$

Subtract.

16	10	16	12	14	16
-9	-8	-8	-6	-8	-7
7					

11	14	15	12	17	10
-7	-9	-9	-8	-8	-5

14	17	13	15	18	13
-7	-9	-7	-8	-9	-8

Perfect score: 36   My score: _____

Problem Solving

Solve each problem.

Michelle has 18 tickets.

She uses 9 of them.

How many tickets are left?

$$\begin{array}{r} 18 \\ -\ 9 \\ \hline 9 \end{array}$$

Jeff buys 14 nails.

He uses 6 of them.

How many are left?

There are 10 people on the train.

7 more get on.

How many people are on the train?

Jim has 13 pencils in his desk.

He takes 4 pencils out of his desk.

How many pencils are left in his desk?

Sally's house has 7 windows in it.

June's house has 9 windows in it.

How many windows do Sally's and June's houses have in all?

Lesson 8   Addition and Subtraction

Add or subtract.

If you get 9, color the part red.
If you get 14, color the part brown.

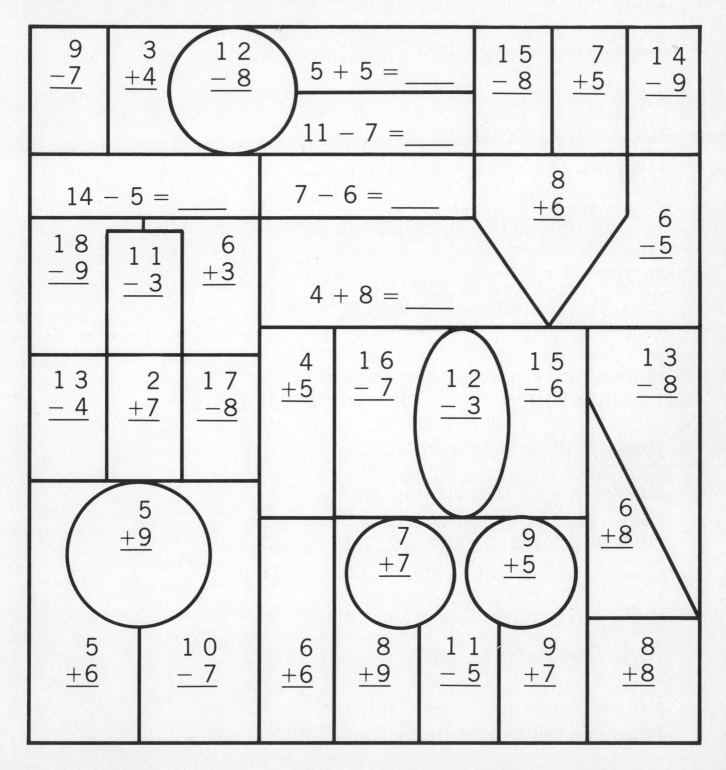

Problem Solving

Solve each problem.

Linda needed 17 balloons for a party.

Linda had 8 balloons at home.

How many more balloons did Linda need?

$$\begin{array}{r} 17 \\ -\ 8 \\ \hline 9 \end{array}$$

Jim had 9 white cowboy hats.

He also had 7 black cowboy hats.

How many cowboy hats did Jim have?

The office helper had 18 letters to write.

She wrote 9.

How many more letters did she have to write?

Dave read 8 books at school.

Jane read 7 books at school.

How many books did Dave and Jane read in all?

Craig had 16 bolts.

He used 8 of the bolts.

How many bolts did Craig have left?

Perfect score: 5   My score: _____

34

NAME _____

Add.

5	6	9	8	5	7
+8	+7	+5	+9	+6	+7

7	9	6	9	8	7
+6	+9	+9	+7	+8	+8

Subtract.

1 2	1 6	1 1	1 3	1 5	1 4
− 7	− 8	− 8	− 9	− 7	− 9

1 8	1 3	1 7	1 4	1 2	1 3
− 9	− 4	− 9	− 5	− 9	− 6

Solve each problem.

_____ tomatoes on vine

_____ tomatoes on ground

_____ tomatoes in all

_____ boots in all

_____ gray boots

_____ blue boots

Perfect score: 26   My score: _____

35

NAME _____

Circle the fraction that tells how much is blue.

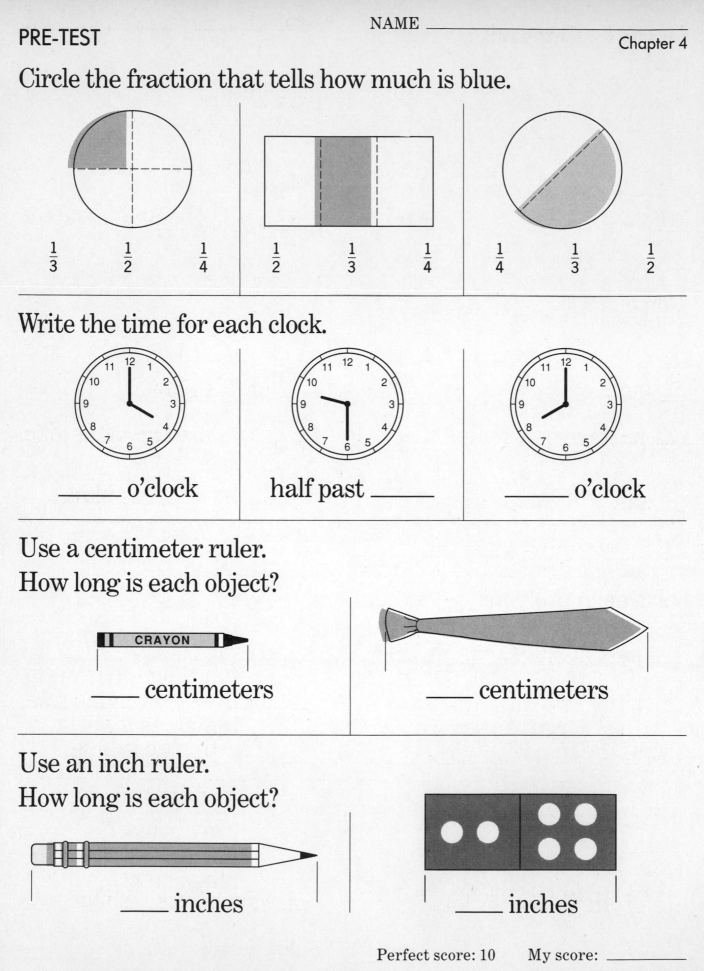

$\frac{1}{3}$ $\frac{1}{2}$ $\frac{1}{4}$

$\frac{1}{2}$ $\frac{1}{3}$ $\frac{1}{4}$

$\frac{1}{4}$ $\frac{1}{3}$ $\frac{1}{2}$

Write the time for each clock.

_____ o'clock

half past _____

_____ o'clock

Use a centimeter ruler.
How long is each object?

CRAYON

_____ centimeters

_____ centimeters

Use an inch ruler.
How long is each object?

_____ inches

_____ inches

Perfect score: 10   My score: _____

Lesson 1 One Half

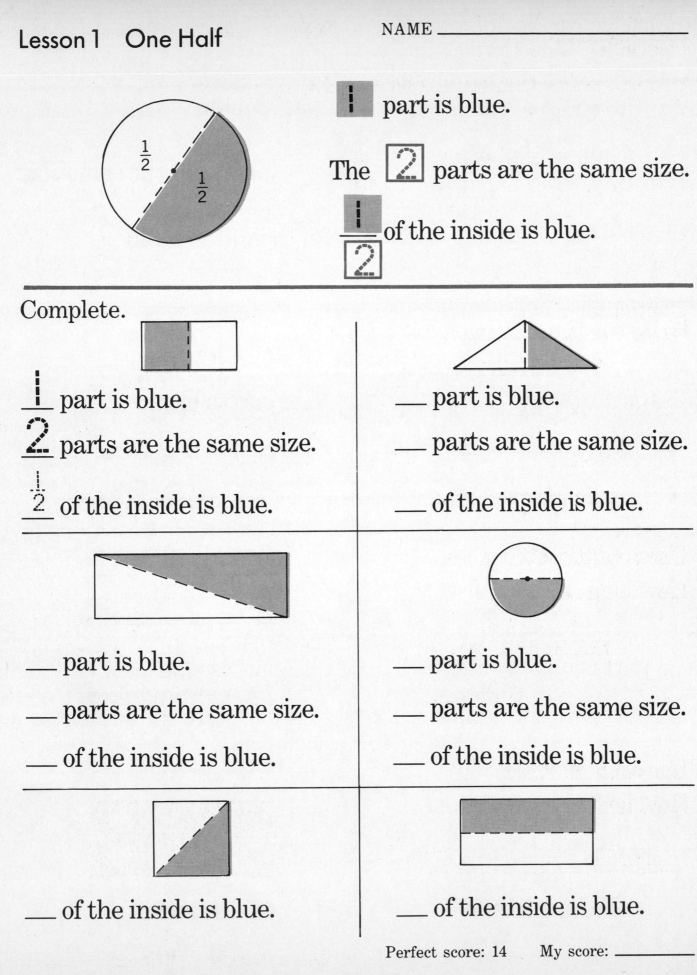

$\frac{1}{2}$ $\frac{1}{2}$

1 part is blue.

The **2** parts are the same size.

$\frac{1}{2}$ of the inside is blue.

Complete.

1 part is blue.

2 parts are the same size.

$\frac{1}{2}$ of the inside is blue.

___ part is blue.

___ parts are the same size.

___ of the inside is blue.

___ part is blue.

___ parts are the same size.

___ of the inside is blue.

___ part is blue.

___ parts are the same size.

___ of the inside is blue.

___ of the inside is blue.

___ of the inside is blue.

Perfect score: 14   My score: _____

Lesson 2   One Third

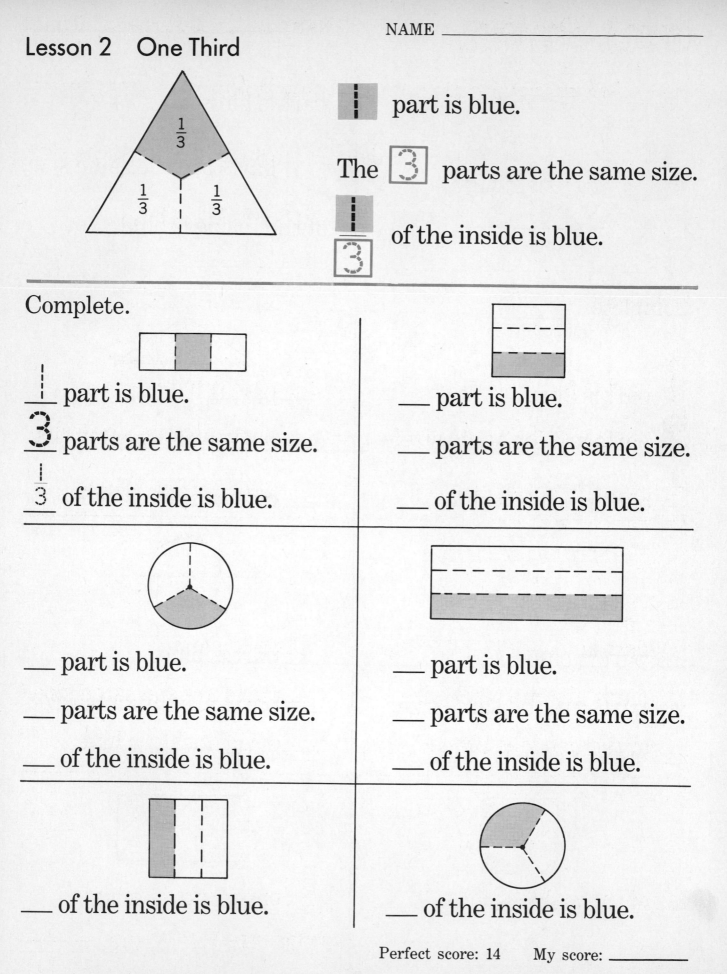

| part is blue. |

The ⟨3⟩ parts are the same size.

$\frac{1}{3}$ of the inside is blue.

Complete.

___ part is blue.

3 parts are the same size.

$\frac{1}{3}$ of the inside is blue.

___ part is blue.

___ parts are the same size.

___ of the inside is blue.

___ part is blue.

___ parts are the same size.

___ of the inside is blue.

___ part is blue.

___ parts are the same size.

___ of the inside is blue.

___ of the inside is blue.

___ of the inside is blue.

Perfect score: 14   My score: _____

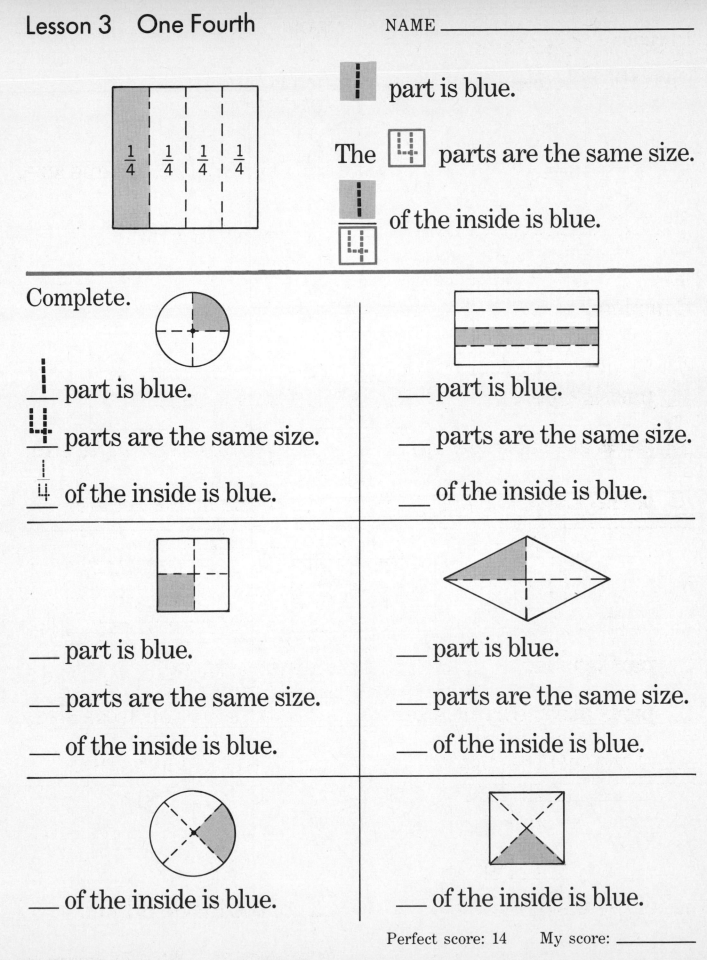

part is blue.

The ⊞ parts are the same size.

$\frac{\blacksquare}{⊞}$ of the inside is blue.

Complete.

$\frac{1}{4}$ part is blue.

parts are the same size.

$\frac{1}{4}$ of the inside is blue.

___ part is blue.

___ parts are the same size.

___ of the inside is blue.

___ part is blue.

___ parts are the same size.

___ of the inside is blue.

___ part is blue.

___ parts are the same size.

___ of the inside is blue.

___ of the inside is blue.

___ of the inside is blue.

Perfect score: 14   My score: _____

Fractions

Ring the fraction that tells how much is blue.

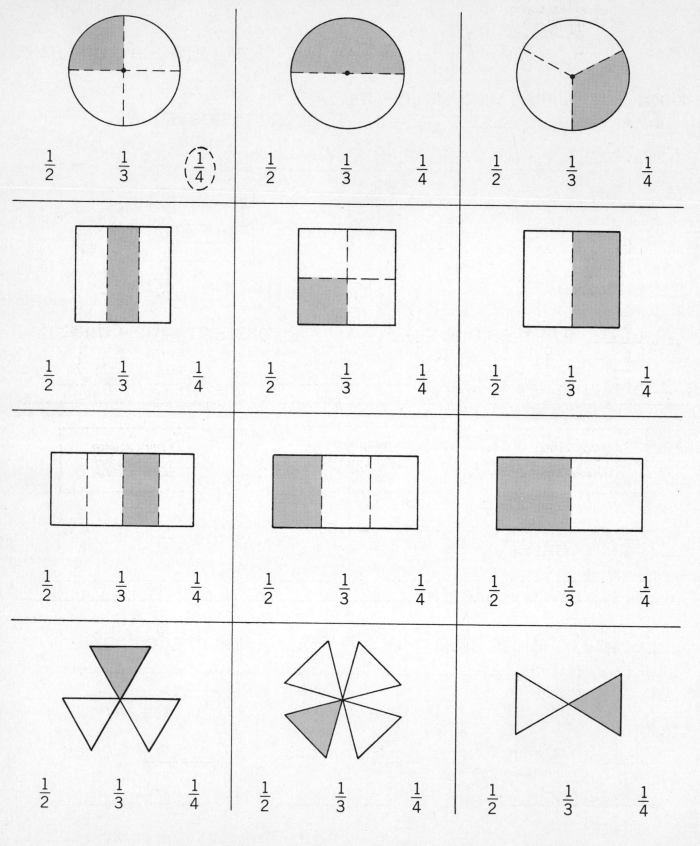

$\frac{1}{2}$ $\frac{1}{3}$ $\left(\frac{1}{4}\right)$	$\frac{1}{2}$ $\frac{1}{3}$ $\frac{1}{4}$	$\frac{1}{2}$ $\frac{1}{3}$ $\frac{1}{4}$
$\frac{1}{2}$ $\frac{1}{3}$ $\frac{1}{4}$	$\frac{1}{2}$ $\frac{1}{3}$ $\frac{1}{4}$	$\frac{1}{2}$ $\frac{1}{3}$ $\frac{1}{4}$
$\frac{1}{2}$ $\frac{1}{3}$ $\frac{1}{4}$	$\frac{1}{2}$ $\frac{1}{3}$ $\frac{1}{4}$	$\frac{1}{2}$ $\frac{1}{3}$ $\frac{1}{4}$
$\frac{1}{2}$ $\frac{1}{3}$ $\frac{1}{4}$	$\frac{1}{2}$ $\frac{1}{3}$ $\frac{1}{4}$	$\frac{1}{2}$ $\frac{1}{3}$ $\frac{1}{4}$

Perfect score: 12   My score: _____

Lesson 4   Time—Hour

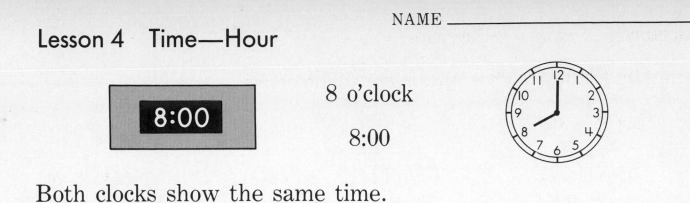

8:00   8 o'clock

8:00

Both clocks show the same time.

___

Write the time for each clock.

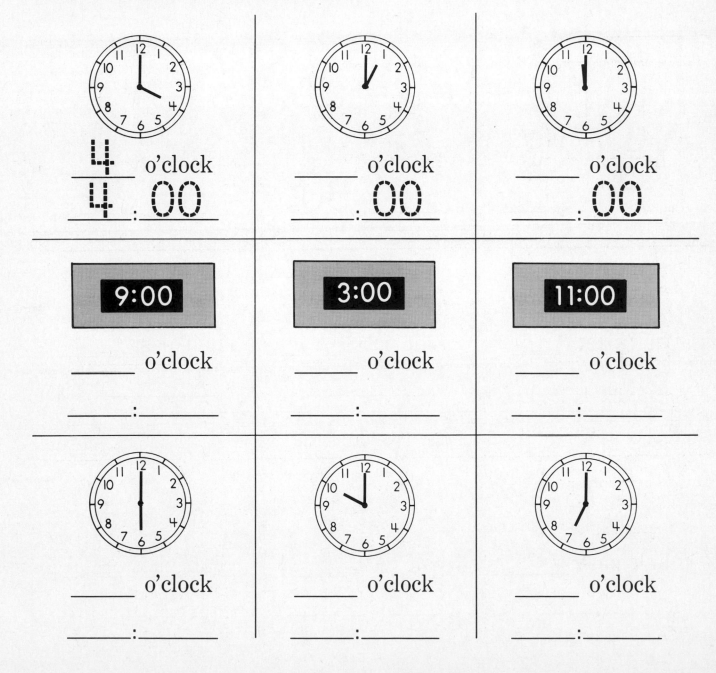

4 o'clock

4:**00**

_____ o'clock

___:**00**

_____ o'clock

___:**00**

9:00

_____ o'clock

___:___

3:00

_____ o'clock

___:___

11:00

_____ o'clock

___:___

_____ o'clock

___:___

_____ o'clock

___:___

_____ o'clock

___:___

Perfect score: 18   My score: _____

Lesson 5   Time—Half Hour

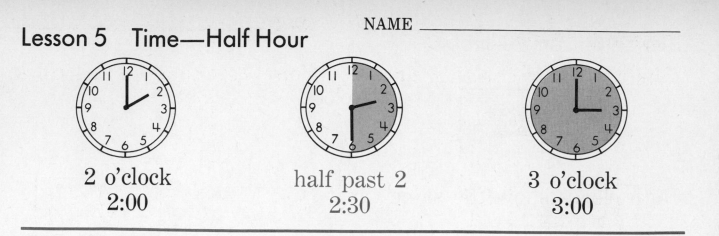

2 o'clock
2:00

half past 2
2:30

3 o'clock
3:00

Write the time for each clock.

half past __3__
__3__ : __30__

half past ____
____ : __30__

half past ____
____ : __30__

10:30

4:30

7:30

half past ____
____ : ____

half past ____
____ : ____

half past ____
____ : ____

half past ____
____ : ____

half past ____
____ : ____

half past ____
____ : ____

Perfect score: 18   My score: _____

42

Lesson 6 Time

Show this time on this clock. Show this time on this clock.

Perfect score: 6   My score: _____

43

Problem Solving

Solve each problem.

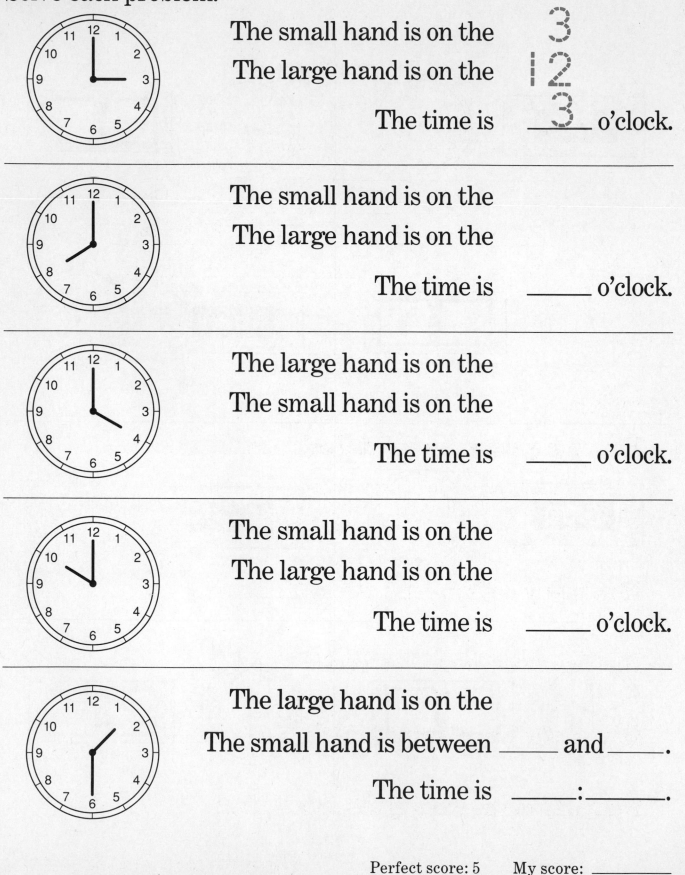

The small hand is on the
The large hand is on the

The time is _____ o'clock.

The small hand is on the
The large hand is on the

The time is _____ o'clock.

The large hand is on the
The small hand is on the

The time is _____ o'clock.

The small hand is on the
The large hand is on the

The time is _____ o'clock.

The large hand is on the
The small hand is between _____ and _____.

The time is _____ : _____.

NAME _____

OCTOBER						
S	M	T	W	T	F	S
1	2	3	4	5	6	7
8	9	10	11	12	13	14
15	16	17	18	19	20	21
22	23	24	25	26	27	28
29	30	31				

Complete.

How many days are in October? _____

How many Saturdays are in October? _____

How many days are in 1 week? _____

How many days are in 2 weeks? _____

How many Tuesdays are in October? _____

What day of the week is the 26th? _____

Perfect score: 6   My score: _____

Calendar

JANUARY							FEBRUARY							MARCH							APRIL						
S	M	T	W	T	F	S	S	M	T	W	T	F	S	S	M	T	W	T	F	S	S	M	T	W	T	F	S
1	2	3	4	5	6	7			1	2	3	4			1	2	3	4							1
8	9	10	11	12	13	14	5	6	7	8	9	10	11	5	6	7	8	9	10	11	2	3	4	5	6	7	8
15	16	17	18	19	20	21	12	13	14	15	16	17	18	12	13	14	15	16	17	18	9	10	11	12	13	14	15
22	23	24	25	26	27	28	19	20	21	22	23	24	25	19	20	21	22	23	24	25	16	17	18	19	20	21	22
29	30	31					26	27	28					26	27	28	29	30	31		23/30	24	25	26	27	28	29

MAY							JUNE							JULY							AUGUST						
S	M	T	W	T	F	S	S	M	T	W	T	F	S	S	M	T	W	T	F	S	S	M	T	W	T	F	S
	1	2	3	4	5	6					1	2	3							1			1	2	3	4	5
7	8	9	10	11	12	13	4	5	6	7	8	9	10	2	3	4	5	6	7	8	6	7	8	9	10	11	12
14	15	16	17	18	19	20	11	12	13	14	15	16	17	9	10	11	12	13	14	15	13	14	15	16	17	18	19
21	22	23	24	25	26	27	18	19	20	21	22	23	24	16	17	18	19	20	21	22	20	21	22	23	24	25	26
28	29	30	31				25	26	27	28	29	30		23/30	24/31	25	26	27	28	29	27	28	29	30	31		

SEPTEMBER							OCTOBER							NOVEMBER							DECEMBER						
S	M	T	W	T	F	S	S	M	T	W	T	F	S	S	M	T	W	T	F	S	S	M	T	W	T	F	S
					1	2	1	2	3	4	5	6	7				1	2	3	4						1	2
3	4	5	6	7	8	9	8	9	10	11	12	13	14	5	6	7	8	9	10	11	3	4	5	6	7	8	9
10	11	12	13	14	15	16	15	16	17	18	19	20	21	12	13	14	15	16	17	18	10	11	12	13	14	15	16
17	18	19	20	21	22	23	22	23	24	25	26	27	28	19	20	21	22	23	24	25	17	18	19	20	21	22	23
24	25	26	27	28	29	30	29	30	31					26	27	28	29	30			24/31	25	26	27	28	29	30

Complete.

How many months are in 1 year? _____

How many months have exactly 30 days? _____

How many months have 31 days? _____

Which month has only 28 days? _____

How many months begin with the letter J? _____

How many months have 5 Saturdays? _____

Perfect score: 6   My score: _____

46

Lesson 8   Centimeter

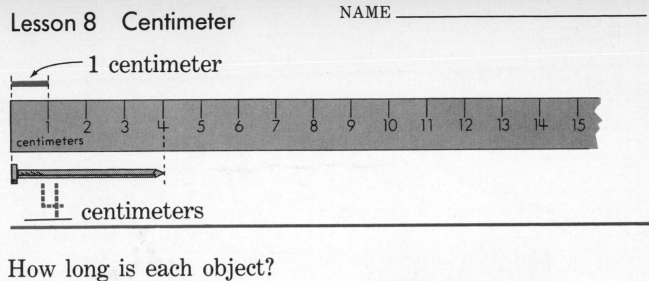

1 centimeter

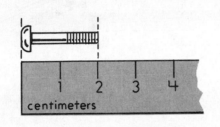

_4_ centimeters

How long is each object?

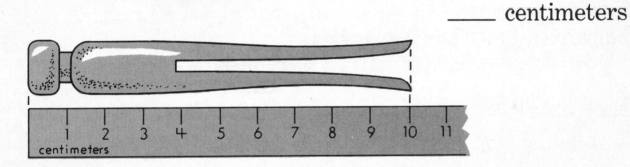

_____ centimeters

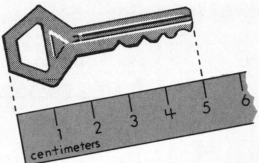

_____ centimeters

_____ centimeters

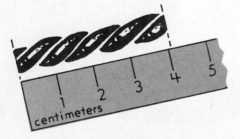

_____ centimeters

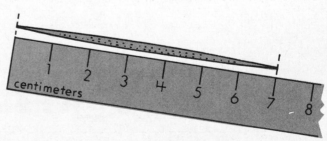

_____ centimeters

Perfect score: 5   My score: _____

47

Centimeter

← Cut off this ruler.

How long is each object?

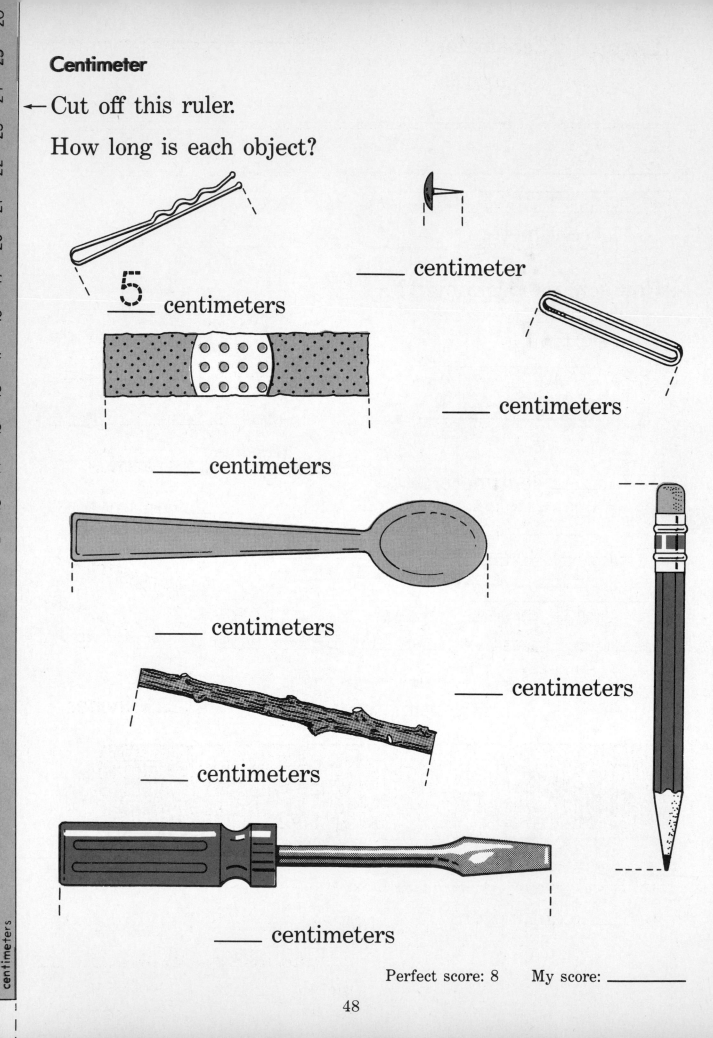

5 centimeters

____ centimeter

____ centimeters

____ centimeters

____ centimeters

____ centimeters

____ centimeters

____ centimeters

Perfect score: 8   My score: _____

48

Lesson 9　Inch

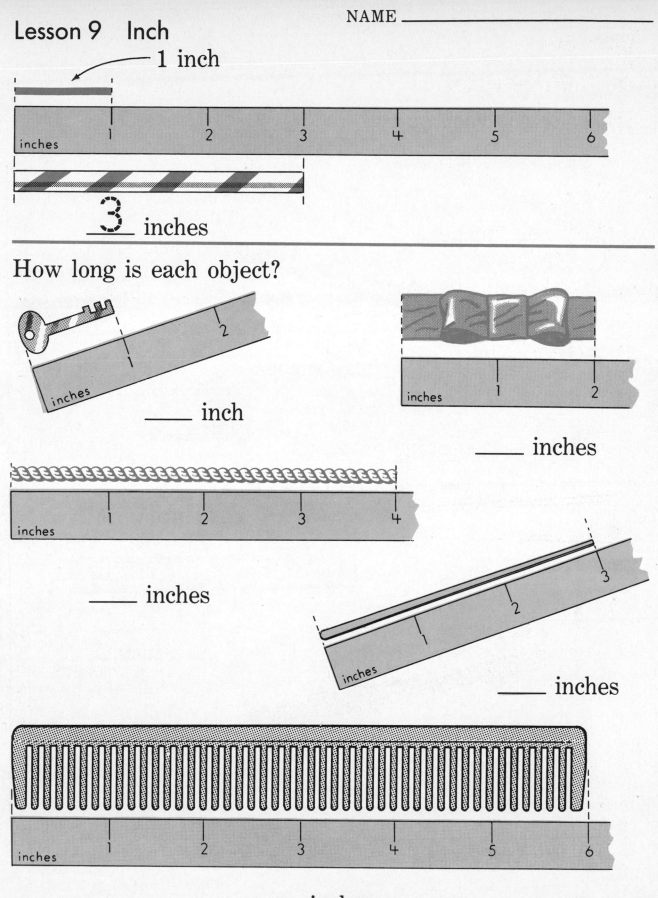

1 inch

__3__ inches

How long is each object?

_____ inch

_____ inches

_____ inches

_____ inches

_____ inches

Perfect score: 5　My score: _____

49

Inch

← Cut off this ruler.

How long is each object?

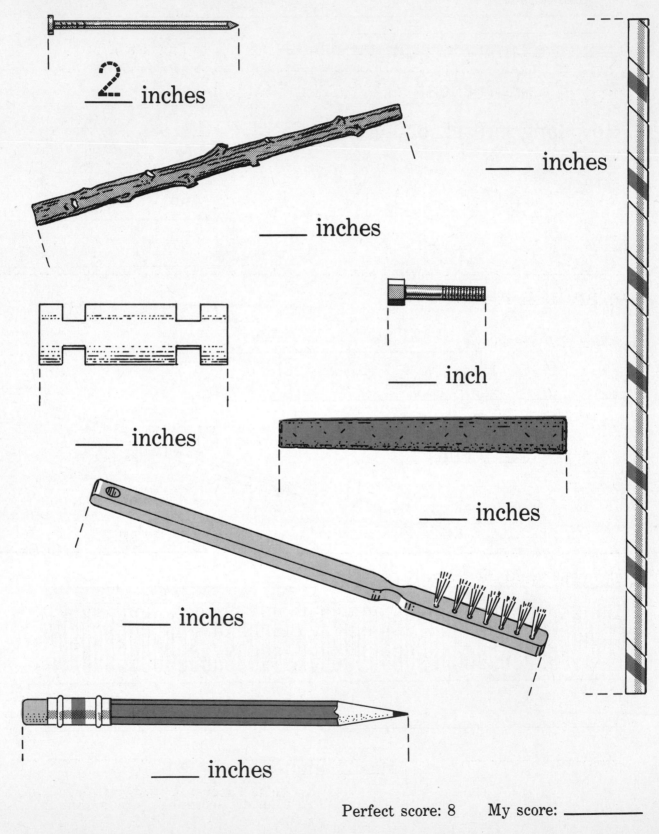

_2_ inches

____ inches

____ inches

____ inches

____ inch

____ inches

____ inches

____ inches

Perfect score: 8   My score: _____

50

Chapter 4 Checkup

Use a centimeter ruler.

How long is each object?

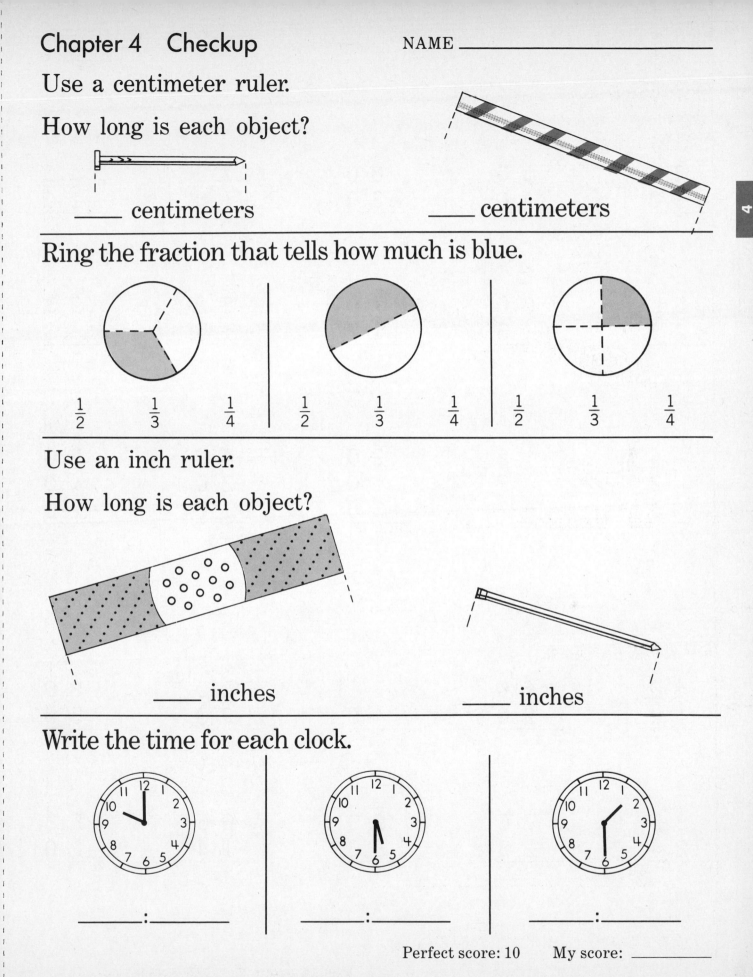

_____ centimeters

_____ centimeters

Ring the fraction that tells how much is blue.

$\frac{1}{2}$ $\frac{1}{3}$ $\frac{1}{4}$ | $\frac{1}{2}$ $\frac{1}{3}$ $\frac{1}{4}$ | $\frac{1}{2}$ $\frac{1}{3}$ $\frac{1}{4}$

Use an inch ruler.

How long is each object?

_____ inches

_____ inches

Write the time for each clock.

_____ : _____   _____ : _____   _____ : _____

Perfect score: 10   My score: _____

51

PRE-TEST

Add.

20 +30	30 +40	60 +30	70 +10	40 +10

55 +23	60 +15	70 +12	82 +15	93 + 3

4 2 +1	2 2 +2	20 10 +30	40 20 +10	30 40 +20

Subtract.

40 −10	60 −20	70 −40	30 −20	80 −50

85 −24	76 −23	99 −33	65 −14	53 −20

Lesson 1 Addition and Subtraction Review

Add.

9 +8	6 +6	7 +9	5 +7	9 +9	4 +8
7 +6	6 +9	8 +6	7 +7	5 +8	8 +2
9 +4	7 +8	5 +5	9 +1	3 +9	5 +6

Subtract.

1 8 − 9	1 1 − 9	1 0 − 5	1 2 − 4	1 3 − 7	1 4 − 9
1 0 − 6	1 2 − 7	1 3 − 5	1 1 − 3	1 5 − 8	1 0 − 9
1 4 − 7	1 1 − 6	1 5 − 7	1 7 − 9	1 2 − 8	1 3 − 4

Perfect score: 36   My score: _____

Addition and Subtraction Review

Ring each name for the number in the ◯.

(11)

4 + 8

(5 + 6)

(4 + 7)

(9 + 2)

(8 + 3)

6 + 6

(16)

5 + 7

8 + 7

6 + 9

7 + 9

9 + 7

8 + 8

(15)

7 + 7

8 + 7

7 + 8

6 + 9

5 + 9

9 + 6

(13)

8 + 5

6 + 8

9 + 4

7 + 6

9 + 5

6 + 7

4 + 8

(7)

17 − 8

15 − 8

13 − 6

16 − 9

14 − 7

14 − 6

(8)

17 − 9

15 − 7

10 − 6

12 − 4

13 − 5

11 − 7

11 − 3

(6)

13 − 7

15 − 6

12 − 6

14 − 8

16 − 7

12 − 8

(9)

17 − 9

16 − 7

15 − 7

13 − 4

11 − 5

12 − 8

18 − 9

Perfect score: 30   My score: _____

54

Lesson 2   Adding Tens

3 tens	3 0	6 tens	6 0
+4 tens	+4 0	+2 tens	+2 0
7 tens	7 0	8 tens	80

Add.

2 tens	2 0	5 tens	5 0
+4 tens	+4 0	+3 tens	+3 0
tens		tens	

2 0	1 0	4 0	3 0	5 0
+2 0	+5 0	+2 0	+4 0	+3 0

3 0	6 0	2 0	7 0	1 0
+2 0	+1 0	+5 0	+1 0	+1 0

1 0	4 0	8 0	6 0	2 0
+2 0	+4 0	+1 0	+3 0	+6 0

7 0	4 0	3 0	5 0	3 0
+2 0	+1 0	+1 0	+4 0	+3 0

Perfect score: 24   My score: _____

Problem Solving

Solve each problem.

There are 20 men in the plane.

30 women get in the plane.

$$\begin{array}{r} 20 \\ +30 \\ \hline \end{array}$$

How many men and women are in the plane?

Jill buys 10 apples.

Carol buys 20 apples.

How many apples in all?

There are 30 ears of corn in one pile.

There are 50 ears of corn in another pile.

How many ears of corn in all?

Henry cut 40 pieces of wood.

Art cut 20 pieces of wood.

How many pieces of wood were cut?

Adolpho had 60 baseball cards.

Maria had 30 baseball cards.

How many baseball cards in all?

Perfect score: 5   My score: _____

Lesson 3   Addition

Join the pennies.
Add the ones.

Join the dimes.
Add the tens.

$$\begin{array}{r} 34 \\ +23 \\ \hline 7 \end{array}$$

$$\begin{array}{r} 34 \\ +23 \\ \hline 57 \end{array}$$

Add.

$$\begin{array}{r} 23 \\ +14 \\ \hline 37 \end{array}$$

Add the ones.
Add the tens.

$$\begin{array}{r} 55 \\ +\ 2 \\ \hline \end{array}$$

$$\begin{array}{r} 70 \\ +23 \\ \hline \end{array}$$

$$\begin{array}{r} 60 \\ +13 \\ \hline \end{array}$$

$$\begin{array}{r} 43 \\ +52 \\ \hline \end{array}$$

$$\begin{array}{r} 36 \\ +21 \\ \hline \end{array}$$

$$\begin{array}{r} 45 \\ +13 \\ \hline \end{array}$$

$$\begin{array}{r} 83 \\ +12 \\ \hline \end{array}$$

$$\begin{array}{r} 26 \\ +43 \\ \hline \end{array}$$

$$\begin{array}{r} 53 \\ +42 \\ \hline \end{array}$$

$$\begin{array}{r} 38 \\ +31 \\ \hline \end{array}$$

$$\begin{array}{r} 81 \\ +\ 3 \\ \hline \end{array}$$

$$\begin{array}{r} 33 \\ +53 \\ \hline \end{array}$$

$$\begin{array}{r} 75 \\ +22 \\ \hline \end{array}$$

$$\begin{array}{r} 71 \\ +27 \\ \hline \end{array}$$

$$\begin{array}{r} 62 \\ +14 \\ \hline \end{array}$$

$$\begin{array}{r} 67 \\ +22 \\ \hline \end{array}$$

$$\begin{array}{r} 43 \\ +46 \\ \hline \end{array}$$

$$\begin{array}{r} 34 \\ +30 \\ \hline \end{array}$$

$$\begin{array}{r} 31 \\ +50 \\ \hline \end{array}$$

$$\begin{array}{r} 60 \\ +32 \\ \hline \end{array}$$

$$\begin{array}{r} 54 \\ +20 \\ \hline \end{array}$$

$$\begin{array}{r} 47 \\ +30 \\ \hline \end{array}$$

$$\begin{array}{r} 40 \\ +40 \\ \hline \end{array}$$

Perfect score: 24   My score: _____

Problem Solving

Solve each problem.

Pablo sees 25 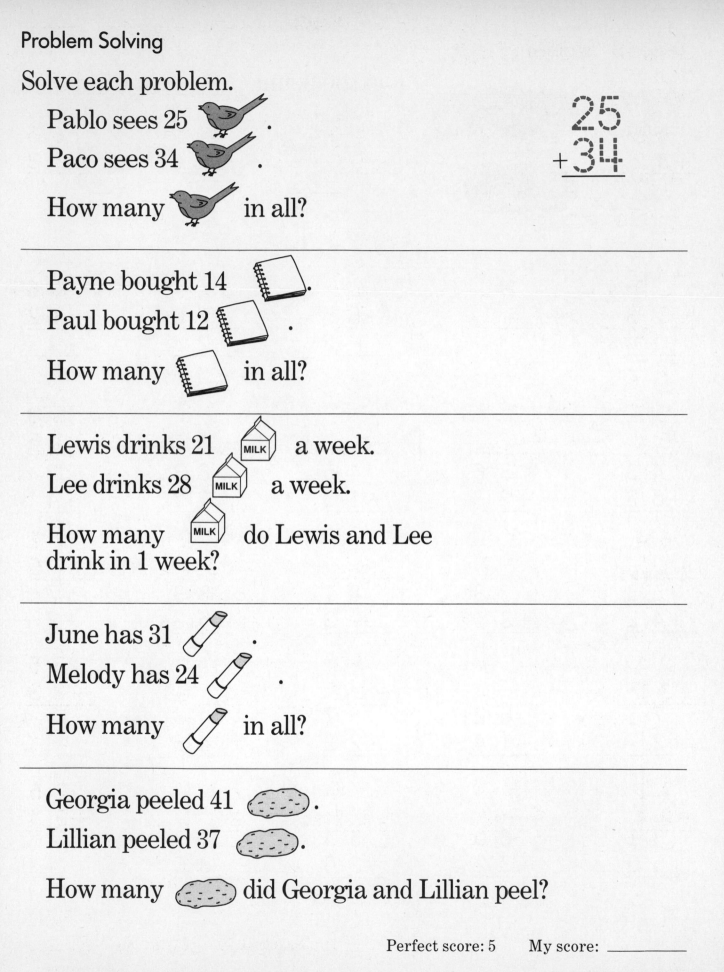 .

Paco sees 34 .

How many in all?

$$\begin{array}{r} 25 \\ +\ 34 \\ \hline \end{array}$$

Payne bought 14 .

Paul bought 12 .

How many in all?

Lewis drinks 21 MILK a week.

Lee drinks 28 MILK a week.

How many MILK do Lewis and Lee drink in 1 week?

June has 31 .

Melody has 24 .

How many in all?

Georgia peeled 41 .

Lillian peeled 37 .

How many did Georgia and Lillian peel?

Perfect score: 5   My score: _____

58

Lesson 4   Addition (2 digit)

Add.

$$
\begin{array}{r} 45 \\ +32 \\ \hline 77 \end{array}
\qquad
\begin{array}{r} 52 \\ +24 \\ \hline 76 \end{array}
\qquad
\begin{array}{r} 40 \\ +10 \\ \hline \end{array}
\qquad
\begin{array}{r} 22 \\ +22 \\ \hline \end{array}
\qquad
\begin{array}{r} 65 \\ +13 \\ \hline \end{array}
$$

$$
\begin{array}{r} 14 \\ +51 \\ \hline \end{array}
\qquad
\begin{array}{r} 18 \\ +41 \\ \hline \end{array}
\qquad
\begin{array}{r} 63 \\ +31 \\ \hline \end{array}
\qquad
\begin{array}{r} 34 \\ +51 \\ \hline \end{array}
\qquad
\begin{array}{r} 46 \\ +32 \\ \hline \end{array}
$$

$$
\begin{array}{r} 23 \\ +54 \\ \hline \end{array}
\qquad
\begin{array}{r} 44 \\ +42 \\ \hline \end{array}
\qquad
\begin{array}{r} 62 \\ +35 \\ \hline \end{array}
\qquad
\begin{array}{r} 73 \\ +25 \\ \hline \end{array}
\qquad
\begin{array}{r} 80 \\ +15 \\ \hline \end{array}
$$

$$
\begin{array}{r} 64 \\ +15 \\ \hline \end{array}
\qquad
\begin{array}{r} 15 \\ +22 \\ \hline \end{array}
\qquad
\begin{array}{r} 33 \\ +33 \\ \hline \end{array}
\qquad
\begin{array}{r} 82 \\ +17 \\ \hline \end{array}
\qquad
\begin{array}{r} 71 \\ +25 \\ \hline \end{array}
$$

$$
\begin{array}{r} 26 \\ +33 \\ \hline \end{array}
\qquad
\begin{array}{r} 18 \\ +31 \\ \hline \end{array}
\qquad
\begin{array}{r} 43 \\ +12 \\ \hline \end{array}
\qquad
\begin{array}{r} 24 \\ +24 \\ \hline \end{array}
\qquad
\begin{array}{r} 55 \\ +23 \\ \hline \end{array}
$$

$$
\begin{array}{r} 72 \\ +24 \\ \hline \end{array}
\qquad
\begin{array}{r} 66 \\ +32 \\ \hline \end{array}
\qquad
\begin{array}{r} 54 \\ +11 \\ \hline \end{array}
\qquad
\begin{array}{r} 11 \\ +11 \\ \hline \end{array}
\qquad
\begin{array}{r} 25 \\ +24 \\ \hline \end{array}
$$

Perfect score: 30   My score: _____

Problem Solving

Ken has	Jill has	Pam has	Rod has
25¢	26¢	20¢	32¢

Complete.

Who has the most money? _____

Who has the least money? _____

Solve each problem.

Ken has	25¢	Pam has	20¢
Pam has	+ 20¢	Rod has	+ 32¢
Ken and Pam have	45¢	Pam and Rod have	¢

Jill has	¢	Rod has	¢
Pam has	+ ¢	Jill has	+ ¢
Jill and Pam have	¢	Rod and Jill have	¢

Ken has	¢	Pam has	¢
Rod has	+ ¢	Ken has	+ ¢
Ken and Rod have	¢	Pam and Ken have	¢

Perfect score: 8   My score: _____

60

Lesson 5   Subtracting Tens

6 tens	6 0	8 tens	8 0
−3 tens	−3 0	−2 tens	−2 0
3 tens	3 0	6 tens	*60*

Subtract.

7 tens	7 0	4 tens	4 0
−5 tens	−5 0	−2 tens	−2 0
tens		tens	

5 0	6 0	2 0	8 0	4 0
−3 0	−2 0	−1 0	−4 0	−4 0

9 0	8 0	7 0	3 0	5 0
−5 0	−2 0	−3 0	−2 0	−4 0

6 0	4 0	8 0	9 0	7 0
−3 0	−1 0	−3 0	−2 0	−5 0

8 0	9 0	7 0	6 0	5 0
−7 0	−8 0	−4 0	−4 0	−2 0

Perfect score: 24   My score: _____

Problem Solving

Solve each problem.

Mr. Cobb counts 70 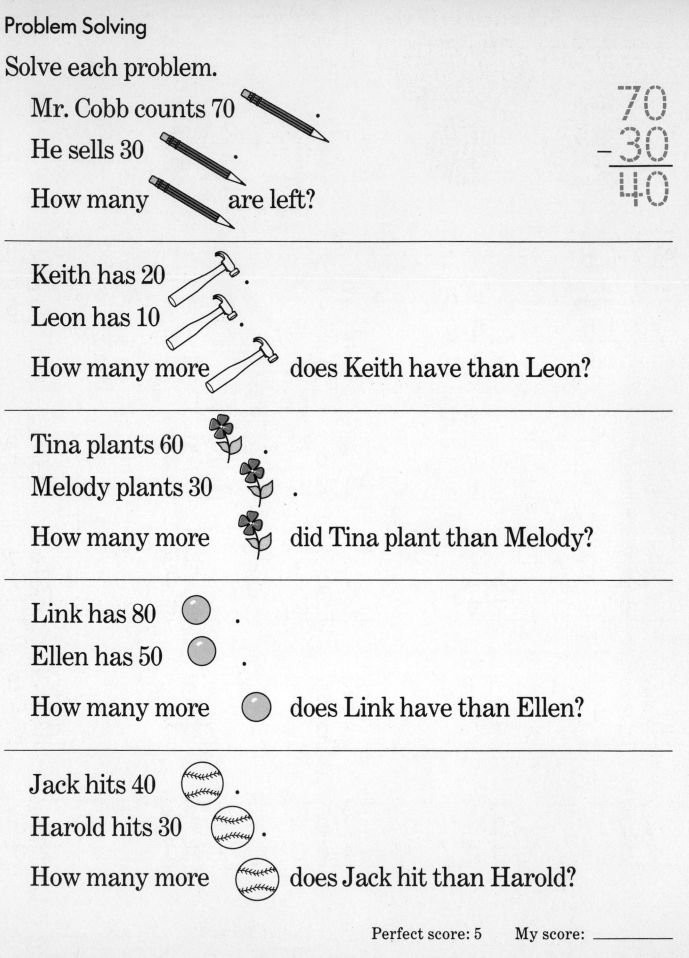 .

He sells 30 .

How many are left?

$$\begin{array}{r} 70 \\ -30 \\ \hline 40 \end{array}$$

Keith has 20 .

Leon has 10 .

How many more does Keith have than Leon?

Tina plants 60 .

Melody plants 30 .

How many more did Tina plant than Melody?

Link has 80 .

Ellen has 50 .

How many more does Link have than Ellen?

Jack hits 40 .

Harold hits 30 .

How many more does Jack hit than Harold?

Perfect score: 5   My score: _____

62

Lesson 6   Subtraction (2 digit)

Take away 1 penny.
Subtract the ones.

$$\begin{array}{r} 53 \\ -21 \\ \hline 2 \end{array}$$

Take away 2 dimes.
Subtract the tens.

$$\begin{array}{r} 53 \\ -21 \\ \hline 32 \end{array}$$

Subtract.

$$\begin{array}{r} 79 \\ -\ 6 \\ \hline 73 \end{array}$$

└─ Subtract the ones.
└── Subtract the tens.

$$\begin{array}{r} 82 \\ -52 \\ \hline 30 \end{array}$$

$$\begin{array}{r} 65 \\ -24 \\ \hline \end{array}$$

$$\begin{array}{r} 56 \\ -26 \\ \hline \end{array}$$

$$\begin{array}{r} 87 \\ -23 \\ \hline \end{array}$$

$$\begin{array}{r} 36 \\ -20 \\ \hline \end{array}$$

$$\begin{array}{r} 94 \\ -\ 1 \\ \hline \end{array}$$

$$\begin{array}{r} 58 \\ -17 \\ \hline \end{array}$$

$$\begin{array}{r} 65 \\ -51 \\ \hline \end{array}$$

$$\begin{array}{r} 57 \\ -10 \\ \hline \end{array}$$

$$\begin{array}{r} 89 \\ -64 \\ \hline \end{array}$$

$$\begin{array}{r} 46 \\ -\ 3 \\ \hline \end{array}$$

$$\begin{array}{r} 75 \\ -15 \\ \hline \end{array}$$

$$\begin{array}{r} 37 \\ -24 \\ \hline \end{array}$$

$$\begin{array}{r} 46 \\ -34 \\ \hline \end{array}$$

$$\begin{array}{r} 78 \\ -68 \\ \hline \end{array}$$

$$\begin{array}{r} 29 \\ -\ 2 \\ \hline \end{array}$$

$$\begin{array}{r} 85 \\ -43 \\ \hline \end{array}$$

$$\begin{array}{r} 78 \\ -21 \\ \hline \end{array}$$

$$\begin{array}{r} 79 \\ -61 \\ \hline \end{array}$$

$$\begin{array}{r} 97 \\ -65 \\ \hline \end{array}$$

$$\begin{array}{r} 84 \\ -\ 2 \\ \hline \end{array}$$

$$\begin{array}{r} 65 \\ -22 \\ \hline \end{array}$$

$$\begin{array}{r} 99 \\ -37 \\ \hline \end{array}$$

Perfect score: 24   My score: _____

Problem Solving

Solve each problem.

Maria has	Pedro has	Madra has	Leroy has
45¢	42¢	65¢	32¢

Solve each problem.

Madra has	**65**¢	Maria has	¢
Pedro has	**−42**¢	Pedro has	− ¢
Madra has this much more	**23**¢	Maria has this much more.	¢

Pedro has	¢	Madra has	¢
Leroy has	− ¢	Leroy has	− ¢
Pedro has this much more.	¢	Madra has this much more.	¢

Madra has	¢	Maria has	¢
Maria has	− ¢	Leroy has	− ¢
Madra has this much more.	¢	Maria has this much more.	¢

Perfect score: 6   My score: _____

64

Lesson 7   Adding Three Numbers

Add the ones.   Add the tens.

$$\begin{array}{r}12 \\ 53 \\ +24 \\ \hline 9\end{array}\Rightarrow \begin{array}{r}12 \\ 53 \\ +24 \\ \hline 89\end{array}$$

12 ⟍
53 ⟶ 5
+24 ⟍ +4
9

60 ⟵ 12
+20 ⟍ 53
⟍ +24
89

Add.

1.	2.	3.	4.	2.	3.
6	4	5	1	2	3
+1	+2	+0	+4	+5	+3
8					

30	20	20	30	40
10	30	20	20	30
+10	+10	+20	+ 0	+10
50				

31	14	66	15	41
16	10	20	51	14
+11	+11	+13	+ 1	+12
58				

33	31	54	71	32
21	12	12	17	21
+23	+51	+21	+ 1	+32

Perfect score: 21   My score: _____

65

Adding Three Numbers

Why did the bird fly south?

A	F	I	K	L	O	R	S	T	W
7	9	35	39	47	58	59	68	86	88

Add. Write the letter for each answer.

$$\begin{array}{r} 1\,2 \\ 1\,2 \\ +1\,1 \\ \hline 35 \end{array} \qquad \begin{array}{r} 4\,3 \\ 2\,2 \\ +2\,1 \\ \hline \end{array} \qquad\qquad \begin{array}{r} 3\,0 \\ 2\,4 \\ +3\,4 \\ \hline \end{array} \qquad \begin{array}{r} 3 \\ 2 \\ +2 \\ \hline \end{array} \qquad \begin{array}{r} 2\,5 \\ 3\,1 \\ +1\,2 \\ \hline \end{array}$$

I

$$\begin{array}{r} 5\,1 \\ 2\,4 \\ +1\,1 \\ \hline \end{array} \qquad \begin{array}{r} 1\,6 \\ 2\,0 \\ +2\,2 \\ \hline \end{array} \qquad \begin{array}{r} 3\,1 \\ 1\,6 \\ +1\,1 \\ \hline \end{array} \qquad\qquad \begin{array}{r} 3 \\ 3 \\ +3 \\ \hline \end{array} \qquad \begin{array}{r} 1 \\ 2 \\ +4 \\ \hline \end{array} \qquad \begin{array}{r} 1\,3 \\ 2\,4 \\ +2\,2 \\ \hline \end{array}$$

$$\begin{array}{r} 6\,3 \\ 1\,0 \\ +1\,3 \\ \hline \end{array} \qquad \begin{array}{r} 3\,0 \\ 1\,7 \\ +1\,1 \\ \hline \end{array} \qquad\qquad \begin{array}{r} 5\,1 \\ 2\,6 \\ +1\,1 \\ \hline \end{array} \qquad \begin{array}{r} 3 \\ 3 \\ +1 \\ \hline \end{array} \qquad \begin{array}{r} 1\,4 \\ 2\,3 \\ +1\,0 \\ \hline \end{array} \qquad \begin{array}{r} 1\,3 \\ 1\,1 \\ +1\,5 \\ \hline \end{array}$$

Perfect score: 34   My score: _____

Lesson 8   Money

half dollar

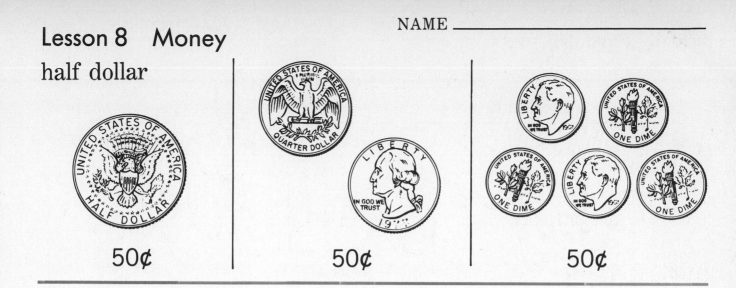

50¢   50¢   50¢

Tell how many cents there are.

$$\begin{array}{r} 50¢ \\ +25¢ \\ \hline 75¢ \end{array}$$

$$\begin{array}{r} 50¢ \\ +30¢ \\ \hline ¢ \end{array}$$

$$\begin{array}{r} ¢ \\ + ¢ \\ \hline ¢ \end{array}$$

$$\begin{array}{r} ¢ \\ + ¢ \\ \hline ¢ \end{array}$$

$$\begin{array}{r} 50¢ \\ 25¢ \\ +10¢ \\ \hline ¢ \end{array}$$

$$\begin{array}{r} ¢ \\ ¢ \\ + ¢ \\ \hline ¢ \end{array}$$

Perfect score: 6   My score: _____

Problem Solving

Comb — 30¢ Toothbrush — 34¢ Tooth Paste — 25¢

Solve each problem.

You buy a [comb] and a [toothbrush].
$$\begin{array}{r} 30¢ \\ + 34¢ \\ \hline \end{array}$$
You spent ____ ¢

You have $$\begin{array}{r} 50¢ \\ - 30¢ \\ \hline \end{array}$$
You buy a [comb].
You have left ____ ¢

You buy a [toothbrush] and [Tooth Paste].
$$\begin{array}{r} ¢ \\ + \quad ¢ \\ \hline \end{array}$$
You spent ____ ¢

You have $$\begin{array}{r} 89¢ \\ - \quad ¢ \\ \hline \end{array}$$
You buy a [Tooth Paste].
You have left ____ ¢

You buy a [comb] and [Tooth Paste].
$$\begin{array}{r} ¢ \\ + \quad ¢ \\ \hline \end{array}$$
You spent ____ ¢

You have $$\begin{array}{r} 97¢ \\ - \quad ¢ \\ \hline \end{array}$$
You buy a [toothbrush].
You have left ____ ¢

Perfect score: 6   My score: _____

68

Lesson 9   Addition and Subtraction

Add.

4 5 +2 2	5 3 +3 4	1 8 +2 1	4 0 +3 0	6 2 +1 6	7 6 +2 3

3 2 +1 6	2 7 +4 0	5 0 +2 0	9 2 + 6	4 2 +3 7	5 1 +2 4

1 1 1 4 +1 0	4 0 1 2 +3 4	2 0 1 6 +2 3	3 5 2 2 +4 0	4 1 3 2 +1 4	1 0 2 0 +3 0

Subtract.

9 4 −1 3	6 6 −3 3	8 8 −4 4	7 3 −2 3	9 9 −8 9	4 4 −3 4

5 9 −4 3	3 7 −1 2	8 6 −4 2	5 6 −3 4	8 0 −7 0	7 5 −5 2

Perfect score: 30   My score: _____

Problem Solving

Solve each problem.

24 frogs in the water.

43 frogs hopping on the land.

How many frogs in all?

$$\begin{array}{r} 24 \\ +43 \\ \hline 67 \end{array}$$

---

60 boys were swimming at the beach.

40 girls came to swim.

How many more boys than girls?

The team shot 55 baskets.

The team missed 24 baskets.

How many baskets did the team make?

There are 44 rows of corn in a field.

There are 53 rows of corn in the other field.

How many rows of corn in all?

Lee pounds 14 posts in the ground.

Damien pounds 23 posts.

Dale pounds 32 posts.

How many posts did the boys pound in the ground?

Perfect score: 5   My score: _____

70

NAME _____

Add.

4 4	6 2	4 0	5 8	7 1	
+2 4	+3 5	+3 0	+4 1	+2 5	+5 3

5	2 5	4 1	3 4	5 2	2 2
2	3 3	5 0	4 2	3 1	4 1
+1	+1 1	+ 4	+1 1	+1 4	+1 5

Subtract.

2 5	7 5	8 6	9 3	6 7	6 0
−1 3	−2 4	−5 3	−2 3	−3 6	−3 0

4 9	4 6	5 8	7 6	8 2	9 5
−3 8	−2 2	−4 3	−3 0	−4 1	−4 4

Solve each problem.

Ryan had 53¢.　　　　　　¢

Corbet had 32¢　　+　　¢

Ryan and Corbet
　had this much.　　　¢

Kelly had 68¢.　　　　　¢

She spent 44¢.　　−　　¢

Kelly had this
　much left.　　　　　¢

Chapter 6

-TEST
Add.

```
  2 3        1 6        1 3        3 7        5 3
+1 9       +1 7       +2 8       +1 8       +3 9
```

```
  4 7        5 7        7 3        4 9        6 4
+2 3       +3 4       +1 8       +1 1       +1 8
```

```
  2 5        2 4        2 6        3 5        5 1
+1 6       +3 7       +1 8       +1 6       +2 9
```

Subtract.

```
  4 2        2 4        3 4        4 4        9 3
-1 8       -1 8       -1 7       -3 5       -7 4
```

```
  8 6        7 5        6 6        5 1        2 2
-3 7       -3 8       -4 9       -2 7       -1 8
```

```
  3 1        4 3        5 2        7 1        8 2
-1 8       -2 4       -3 6       -4 3       -6 6
```

Perfect score: 30   My score: _____

Lesson 1   Addition and Subtraction Review

Add.

4 +9	8 +6	9 +8	7 +6	5 +7	6 +5

9 +6	5 +8	7 +4	9 +9	8 +7	7 +9

3 0 +4 0	2 0 +3 0	4 5 +2 3	5 2 +2 3	6 0 +2 5	8 3 +1 5

Subtract.

1 6 − 7	1 5 − 9	1 3 − 4	1 2 − 7	1 1 − 9	1 7 − 8

1 8 − 9	1 7 − 9	1 6 − 8	1 5 − 8	1 4 − 7	1 6 − 9

4 0 −3 0	6 0 −1 0	8 5 −2 3	7 3 −4 1	9 6 −4 3	5 4 −4 4

Perfect score: 36   My score: _____

Addition and Subtraction Review

Add.

4	9	5	6	7	9
+8	+2	+9	+6	+5	+4

8	7	3	7	6	6
+8	+6	+9	+7	+9	+5

4 0	5 0	7 5	6 6	4 7	3 4
+2 0	+3 0	+2 0	+3 1	+5 1	+2 3

Subtract.

1 7	1 5	1 2	1 3	1 4	1 6
− 9	− 6	− 3	− 7	− 6	− 8

1 5	1 4	1 3	1 5	1 2	1 1
− 7	− 9	− 6	− 7	− 9	− 8

3 0	5 0	6 5	8 7	7 5	6 6
−1 0	−3 0	−3 0	−3 4	−2 3	−4 3

Perfect score: 36   My score: _____

Lesson 2   Addition

Add the ones.   Rename 15 as 10 + 5.   Add the tens.

$$\begin{array}{r} 5\ 6 \\ +2\ 9 \\ \hline \end{array}$$

$$\begin{array}{r} 6 \\ +9 \\ \hline 15 \text{ or } 10 + 5 \end{array}$$

$$\begin{array}{r} 1 \\ 5\ 6 \\ +2\ 9 \\ \hline 5 \end{array}$$

$$\begin{array}{r} 1 \\ 5\ 6 \\ +2\ 9 \\ \hline 8\ 5 \end{array}$$

Add the ones.   Rename 12 as 10 + 2.   Add the tens.

$$\begin{array}{r} 4\ 7 \\ +3\ 5 \\ \hline \end{array}$$

$$\begin{array}{r} 7 \\ +5 \\ \hline 12 \text{ or } 10 + 2 \end{array}$$

$$\begin{array}{r} 1 \\ 4\ 7 \\ +3\ 5 \\ \hline 2 \end{array}$$

$$\begin{array}{r} 1 \\ 4\ 7 \\ +3\ 5 \\ \hline 8\ 2 \end{array}$$

Add.

$$\begin{array}{r} 4\ 5 \\ +2\ 8 \\ \hline 7\ 3 \end{array} \qquad \begin{array}{r} 1\ 3 \\ +1\ 9 \\ \hline 3\ 2 \end{array} \qquad \begin{array}{r} 4\ 8 \\ +3\ 5 \\ \hline \end{array} \qquad \begin{array}{r} 6\ 9 \\ +1\ 8 \\ \hline \end{array} \qquad \begin{array}{r} 5\ 4 \\ +3\ 9 \\ \hline \end{array}$$

$$\begin{array}{r} 4\ 4 \\ +1\ 7 \\ \hline \end{array} \qquad \begin{array}{r} 3\ 7 \\ +1\ 8 \\ \hline \end{array} \qquad \begin{array}{r} 2\ 8 \\ +3\ 6 \\ \hline \end{array} \qquad \begin{array}{r} 7\ 3 \\ +1\ 8 \\ \hline \end{array} \qquad \begin{array}{r} 6\ 6 \\ +2\ 9 \\ \hline \end{array}$$

$$\begin{array}{r} 5\ 2 \\ +3\ 9 \\ \hline \end{array} \qquad \begin{array}{r} 3\ 8 \\ +4\ 7 \\ \hline \end{array} \qquad \begin{array}{r} 6\ 4 \\ +1\ 8 \\ \hline \end{array} \qquad \begin{array}{r} 2\ 9 \\ +4\ 5 \\ \hline \end{array} \qquad \begin{array}{r} 7\ 5 \\ +1\ 7 \\ \hline \end{array}$$

Perfect score: 15   My score: _____

Addition (2 digit)

Add the ones.

$$\begin{array}{r} 3\ 8 \\ +4\ 3 \\ \hline \end{array}$$

$$\begin{array}{r} 8 \\ +3 \\ \hline 11 \text{ or } 10+1 \end{array}$$

Rename 11 as 10 + 1.

$$\begin{array}{r} 1 \\ 3\ 8 \\ +4\ 3 \\ \hline 1 \end{array}$$

Add the tens.

$$\begin{array}{r} 1 \\ 3\ 8 \\ +4\ 3 \\ \hline 8\ 1 \end{array}$$

Add.

$$\begin{array}{r} 1\ 7 \\ +3\ 4 \\ \hline 5\ 1 \end{array}$$
$$\begin{array}{r} 2\ 6 \\ +4\ 7 \\ \hline \end{array}$$
$$\begin{array}{r} 4\ 7 \\ +3\ 5 \\ \hline \end{array}$$
$$\begin{array}{r} 6\ 8 \\ +2\ 4 \\ \hline \end{array}$$
$$\begin{array}{r} 3\ 7 \\ +2\ 8 \\ \hline \end{array}$$

$$\begin{array}{r} 2\ 9 \\ +4\ 8 \\ \hline \end{array}$$
$$\begin{array}{r} 5\ 8 \\ +2\ 7 \\ \hline \end{array}$$
$$\begin{array}{r} 6\ 9 \\ +1\ 7 \\ \hline \end{array}$$
$$\begin{array}{r} 7\ 8 \\ +1\ 3 \\ \hline \end{array}$$
$$\begin{array}{r} 1\ 9 \\ +4\ 4 \\ \hline \end{array}$$

$$\begin{array}{r} 5\ 5 \\ +2\ 8 \\ \hline \end{array}$$
$$\begin{array}{r} 2\ 7 \\ +3\ 5 \\ \hline \end{array}$$
$$\begin{array}{r} 3\ 9 \\ +5\ 2 \\ \hline \end{array}$$
$$\begin{array}{r} 5\ 7 \\ +2\ 7 \\ \hline \end{array}$$
$$\begin{array}{r} 3\ 8 \\ +3\ 6 \\ \hline \end{array}$$

$$\begin{array}{r} 4\ 9 \\ +4\ 3 \\ \hline \end{array}$$
$$\begin{array}{r} 6\ 5 \\ +1\ 8 \\ \hline \end{array}$$
$$\begin{array}{r} 2\ 3 \\ +1\ 8 \\ \hline \end{array}$$
$$\begin{array}{r} 6\ 4 \\ +1\ 8 \\ \hline \end{array}$$
$$\begin{array}{r} 4\ 6 \\ +3\ 9 \\ \hline \end{array}$$

$$\begin{array}{r} 5\ 4 \\ +2\ 7 \\ \hline \end{array}$$
$$\begin{array}{r} 3\ 8 \\ +4\ 4 \\ \hline \end{array}$$
$$\begin{array}{r} 6\ 6 \\ +2\ 6 \\ \hline \end{array}$$
$$\begin{array}{r} 2\ 8 \\ +3\ 4 \\ \hline \end{array}$$
$$\begin{array}{r} 1\ 9 \\ +5\ 6 \\ \hline \end{array}$$

Perfect score: 25   My score: _____

Lesson 3   Addition (2 digit)

Add the ones.   Rename 12 as 10 + 2.   Add the tens.

$$
\begin{array}{r}
6\ 4 \\
+2\ 8 \\
\hline
\end{array}
\qquad
\begin{array}{r}
4 \\
+8 \\
\hline
12\ \text{or}\ 10 + 2
\end{array}
\qquad \Rightarrow \qquad
\begin{array}{r}
1 \\
6\ 4 \\
+2\ 8 \\
\hline
2
\end{array}
\qquad \Rightarrow \qquad
\begin{array}{r}
1 \\
6\ 4 \\
+2\ 8 \\
\hline
9\ 2
\end{array}
$$

Add.

$$
\begin{array}{r}
2\ 8 \\
+1\ 9 \\
\hline
4\ 7
\end{array}
\qquad
\begin{array}{r}
3\ 4 \\
+4\ 9 \\
\hline
\end{array}
\qquad
\begin{array}{r}
2\ 5 \\
+1\ 6 \\
\hline
\end{array}
\qquad
\begin{array}{r}
4\ 6 \\
+2\ 9 \\
\hline
\end{array}
\qquad
\begin{array}{r}
5\ 4 \\
+3\ 9 \\
\hline
\end{array}
$$

$$
\begin{array}{r}
1\ 6 \\
+3\ 9 \\
\hline
\end{array}
\qquad
\begin{array}{r}
6\ 4 \\
+2\ 8 \\
\hline
\end{array}
\qquad
\begin{array}{r}
5\ 8 \\
+2\ 4 \\
\hline
\end{array}
\qquad
\begin{array}{r}
3\ 9 \\
+1\ 7 \\
\hline
\end{array}
\qquad
\begin{array}{r}
3\ 4 \\
+1\ 9 \\
\hline
\end{array}
$$

$$
\begin{array}{r}
5\ 7 \\
+3\ 9 \\
\hline
\end{array}
\qquad
\begin{array}{r}
1\ 4 \\
+4\ 8 \\
\hline
\end{array}
\qquad
\begin{array}{r}
3\ 7 \\
+3\ 9 \\
\hline
\end{array}
\qquad
\begin{array}{r}
6\ 1 \\
+1\ 9 \\
\hline
\end{array}
\qquad
\begin{array}{r}
2\ 9 \\
+4\ 4 \\
\hline
\end{array}
$$

$$
\begin{array}{r}
1\ 7 \\
+3\ 5 \\
\hline
\end{array}
\qquad
\begin{array}{r}
3\ 9 \\
+1\ 4 \\
\hline
\end{array}
\qquad
\begin{array}{r}
4\ 4 \\
+3\ 7 \\
\hline
\end{array}
\qquad
\begin{array}{r}
2\ 5 \\
+4\ 9 \\
\hline
\end{array}
\qquad
\begin{array}{r}
1\ 8 \\
+1\ 8 \\
\hline
\end{array}
$$

$$
\begin{array}{r}
2\ 6 \\
+4\ 8 \\
\hline
\end{array}
\qquad
\begin{array}{r}
3\ 9 \\
+2\ 7 \\
\hline
\end{array}
\qquad
\begin{array}{r}
1\ 4 \\
+2\ 7 \\
\hline
\end{array}
\qquad
\begin{array}{r}
6\ 5 \\
+2\ 5 \\
\hline
\end{array}
\qquad
\begin{array}{r}
5\ 9 \\
+1\ 8 \\
\hline
\end{array}
$$

Perfect score: 25   My score: _____

Problem Solving

Solve each problem.

16 boys ride their bikes to school.

18 girls ride their bikes to school.

How many bikes are ridden to school?

$$\begin{array}{r} 16 \\ +18 \\ \hline 34 \end{array}$$

Dad reads 26 pages.

Mike reads 37 pages.

How many pages did Dad and Mike read?

Mary counts 46 stars.

Mike counts 39 stars.

How many stars did they count?

Mom has 29 golf balls.

Uncle Sam has 43 golf balls.

How many golf balls do they have?

Vicki ran in 26 races.

Kay ran in 14 races.

How many races did they run?

Perfect score: 5   My score: _____

78

Lesson 4 Addition (2 digit)

Add.

3 6 +5 5	1 4 +2 8	5 7 +3 8	4 4 +4 8	3 3 +2 9
2 3 +1 8	2 7 +2 7	6 8 +2 5	2 3 +1 9	4 2 +1 9
5 6 +2 8	4 9 +2 7	3 8 +4 9	3 6 +1 8	4 9 +2 4
1 8 +5 4	5 1 +3 9	7 4 +1 7	3 5 +2 8	5 2 +1 9
4 8 +2 6	2 5 +2 8	3 9 +3 3	2 9 +4 4	5 4 +2 7

Perfect score: 25   My score: _____

Problem Solving

Solve each problem.

Simon sees 36 birds flying.

Julie sees 28 birds flying.

How many birds do they see flying?

$$\begin{array}{r} 36 \\ +28 \\ \hline 64 \end{array}$$

Brandon ran the race in 35 seconds.

Ryan ran the race in 28 seconds.

How many seconds did they run?

Tom has 63 nickels.

Connie has 29 nickels.

How many nickels do they have?

Pam sees 48 monkeys at the zoo.

Brenda sees 35 different monkeys.

How many monkeys did they see?

There are 29 steers in one pen.

There are 47 steers in the other pen.

How many steers in all?

Perfect score: 5   My score: _____

80

Lesson 5   Subtraction (2 digits)

Rename 53 as 4 tens and
13 ones.

```
    4 13
5 3    5̸ 3̸
-2 6   -2 6
```

→ Subtract the ones.

```
    4 13
    5̸ 3̸
   -2 6
       7
```

→ Subtract the tens.

```
    4 13
    5̸ 3̸
   -2 6
     2 7
```

Rename 45 as 3 tens and
15 ones.

```
    3 15
4 5    4̸ 5̸
-1 8   -1 8
```

→ Subtract the ones.

```
    3 15
    4̸ 5̸
   -1 8
       7
```

→ Subtract the tens.

```
    3 15
    4̸ 5̸
   -1 8
     2 7
```

Subtract.

```
5 13
6̸ 3̸
-2 8
 35
```

```
6 14
7̸ 4̸
-3 9
 35
```

```
4 7
-2 8
```

```
5 2
-2 6
```

```
6 4
-3 6
```

```
8 4
-4 7
```

```
9 3
-5 6
```

```
7 1
-2 3
```

```
2 6
-1 8
```

```
6 7
-4 8
```

```
4 4
-2 8
```

```
5 3
-3 7
```

```
8 2
-4 6
```

```
9 4
-6 6
```

```
5 5
-3 9
```

```
8 6
-5 8
```

```
3 4
-1 8
```

```
5 4
-2 9
```

```
7 3
-5 9
```

```
8 6
-6 9
```

Perfect score: 20   My score: _____

Subtraction (2 digit)

Rename 73 as 6 tens and 13 ones.

$$
\begin{array}{r} 7\ 3 \\ -4\ 8 \\ \hline \end{array}
\qquad
\overset{6\ 13}{\begin{array}{r} \not7\ \not3 \\ -4\ 8 \\ \hline \end{array}}
$$

⟹   Subtract the ones.

$$
\overset{6\ 13}{\begin{array}{r} \not7\ \not3 \\ -4\ 8 \\ \hline 5 \end{array}}
$$

⟹   Subtract the tens.

$$
\overset{6\ 13}{\begin{array}{r} \not7\ \not3 \\ -4\ 8 \\ \hline 2\ 5 \end{array}}
$$

Subtract.

$$
\overset{5\ 13}{\begin{array}{r} \not6\ \not3 \\ -4\ 8 \\ \hline 15 \end{array}}
\qquad
\begin{array}{r} 8\ 3 \\ -4\ 5 \\ \hline \end{array}
\qquad
\begin{array}{r} 7\ 4 \\ -2\ 9 \\ \hline \end{array}
\qquad
\begin{array}{r} 9\ 4 \\ -4\ 8 \\ \hline \end{array}
\qquad
\begin{array}{r} 6\ 2 \\ -2\ 5 \\ \hline \end{array}
$$

$$
\begin{array}{r} 4\ 5 \\ -2\ 7 \\ \hline \end{array}
\qquad
\begin{array}{r} 3\ 3 \\ -2\ 4 \\ \hline \end{array}
\qquad
\begin{array}{r} 2\ 4 \\ -1\ 8 \\ \hline \end{array}
\qquad
\begin{array}{r} 8\ 6 \\ -3\ 7 \\ \hline \end{array}
\qquad
\begin{array}{r} 7\ 2 \\ -4\ 8 \\ \hline \end{array}
$$

$$
\begin{array}{r} 3\ 6 \\ -1\ 7 \\ \hline \end{array}
\qquad
\begin{array}{r} 2\ 6 \\ -1\ 8 \\ \hline \end{array}
\qquad
\begin{array}{r} 4\ 3 \\ -1\ 9 \\ \hline \end{array}
\qquad
\begin{array}{r} 6\ 3 \\ -4\ 8 \\ \hline \end{array}
\qquad
\begin{array}{r} 9\ 3 \\ -1\ 8 \\ \hline \end{array}
$$

$$
\begin{array}{r} 8\ 2 \\ -2\ 6 \\ \hline \end{array}
\qquad
\begin{array}{r} 7\ 3 \\ -2\ 8 \\ \hline \end{array}
\qquad
\begin{array}{r} 9\ 5 \\ -6\ 9 \\ \hline \end{array}
\qquad
\begin{array}{r} 5\ 7 \\ -3\ 8 \\ \hline \end{array}
\qquad
\begin{array}{r} 4\ 1 \\ -2\ 5 \\ \hline \end{array}
$$

$$
\begin{array}{r} 5\ 4 \\ -1\ 8 \\ \hline \end{array}
\qquad
\begin{array}{r} 6\ 1 \\ -3\ 4 \\ \hline \end{array}
\qquad
\begin{array}{r} 9\ 1 \\ -3\ 7 \\ \hline \end{array}
\qquad
\begin{array}{r} 8\ 1 \\ -4\ 4 \\ \hline \end{array}
\qquad
\begin{array}{r} 3\ 2 \\ -1\ 5 \\ \hline \end{array}
$$

Perfect score: 25   My score: _____

Lesson 6   Subtraction (2 digit)

Rename 61 as 5 tens and 11 ones.

Subtract the ones.

Subtract the tens.

```
      5 11        5 11                5 11                    5 11
  6 1   6 1                 6̶ 1̶              6̶ 1̶
- 4 3 - 4 3              - 4 3           - 4 3
                                        8               1 8
```

Subtract.

```
  3 17
  4̶ 7̶       7 3       8 4       9 5       6 4
- 2 8     - 4 8     - 6 6     - 1 8     - 2 9
  1 9
```

```
  5 6       3 1       2 5       3 3       4 6
- 3 8     - 1 5     - 1 7     - 1 9     - 2 9
```

```
  9 3       8 2       7 2       4 5       6 1
- 6 4     - 5 5     - 1 4     - 2 8     - 2 3
```

```
  5 1       6 2       3 7       5 0       8 3
- 4 4     - 4 8     - 1 9     - 3 2     - 4 7
```

```
  9 2       8 2       7 6       4 7       7 4
- 7 3     - 7 5     - 3 8     - 2 9     - 3 9
```

Perfect score: 25   My score: _____

Problem Solving

Solve each problem.

Dad cooks 23 potatoes.

He uses 19 potatoes in the potato salad.

How many potatoes are left?

$$\begin{array}{r} {\scriptstyle 1}\ {\scriptstyle 13} \\ 2\!\!\!/3 \\ -19 \\ \hline 4 \end{array}$$

Susan draws 32 butterflies.

She colored 15 of them brown.

How many butterflies does she have left to color?

A book has 66 pages.

Pedro reads 39 pages.

How many pages are left to read?

Jerry picks up 34 sea shells.

He puts 15 of them in a box.

How many does he have left?

Beth buys 72 sheets of paper.

She uses 44 sheets for her school work.

How many sheets of paper are left?

Perfect score: 5   My score: _____

84

NAME _____

Subtract.

8 5	9 3	7 2	6 3	4 3
−1 6	−4 8	−3 5	−2 7	−3 8

5 6	7 5	8 4	9 1	3 7
−2 9	−4 9	−3 8	−6 5	−1 8

2 1	3 5	4 2	7 2	8 1
−1 4	−1 8	−2 9	−4 7	−5 4

6 4	5 3	9 4	4 8	2 3
−3 8	−2 8	−5 7	−3 9	−1 8

7 4	8 3	6 2	5 4	3 2
−5 8	−3 6	−2 6	−2 8	−1 7

Perfect score: 25   My score: _____

Problem Solving

Solve each problem.

Scott has 80 pennies.

Tracy has 45 pennies.

How many pennies in all?

$$\begin{array}{r} 40 \\ +\ 45 \\ \hline 85 \end{array}$$

Mom puts 36 nails in a box.

Edna takes 18 nails out of the box.

How many nails are left in the box?

Liz buys 57 apples and oranges.

29 are oranges.

How many are apples?

Tony can jump a rope 84 times.

Curt can jump a rope 69 times.

How many more times can Tony jump than Curt?

The team scored 74 points.

Michelle scored 37 of the points.

How many points did the rest of the team score?

Perfect score: 5   My score: _____

86

Lesson 8   Addition and Subtraction (2 digit)

Add.

6 4 +2 9	3 7 +4 6	2 4 +1 9	7 1 +1 9	4 9 +1 8
2 7 +4 4	3 3 +1 8	2 8 +2 5	5 9 +1 6	3 4 +4 8
4 3 +2 9	2 6 +4 5	7 2 +1 9	6 9 +1 5	1 8 +3 9

Subtract.

7 6 −4 8	6 7 −5 9	8 8 −6 9	9 3 −4 8	4 5 −2 7
8 4 −1 6	9 5 −2 7	3 6 −1 8	6 3 −2 8	7 2 −4 9
9 1 −3 2	7 2 −4 5	6 2 −1 8	5 4 −3 6	3 3 −1 9

Perfect score: 30   My score: _____

Problem Solving

Solve each problem.

Mr. Smith milks 64 🐄 .

Mr. Jones milks 29 🐄 .

How many more 🐄 does Mr. Smith milk than Mr. Jones?

$$\begin{array}{r} {\scriptstyle 5\ 14} \\ \cancel{6}\cancel{4} \\ -29 \\ \hline 35 \end{array}$$

There are 13 girls playing ⚾ .

18 more girls join in to play.

How many girls are playing ⚾ ?

Sally served the ⚽ 34 times.

Jeff served the ⚽ 19 times.

How many more times did Sally serve?

---

62 red 🌹 grew in the garden.

29 yellow 🌹 grew there too.

How many 🌹 grew in the garden?

Jon has 62 🔩 .

He hammers 45 🔩 in the board.

How many 🔩 does Jon have left?

Perfect score: 5   My score: _____

NAME _____

Add.

2 4	5 6	4 9	6 2	3 9
+1 8	+2 7	+2 6	+1 9	+1 8

2 8	7 3	6 4	5 9	1 3
+3 4	+1 9	+1 8	+3 3	+1 8

Subtract.

5 3	7 6	9 7	6 2	4 4
−2 7	−4 7	−7 8	−3 8	−2 6

8 4	3 8	2 5	8 2	9 6
−3 9	−2 9	−1 8	−4 8	−7 9

Solve each problem.

There are 26 pieces of chalk on the chalkboard.

18 pieces fall on the floor.   − ____

How many pieces are still on the chalkboard?

_____

Jason did 26 pages of homework.

Beth did 36 pages of homework.   + ____

How many pages of homework did they do in all?

PRE-TEST

Write the numerals.

5 hundreds 3 tens 2 ones	8 hundreds 4 tens 1 one
_____	_____
4 hundreds 8 tens 6 ones	3 hundreds 7 tens 8 ones
_____	_____

Add.

```
  3 0 0        6 0 0        2 0 0        5 0 0
+ 1 0 0      + 3 0 0      + 3 0 0      + 2 0 0
```

```
  5 6 9        4 3 2        2 1 5        6 2 6
+ 1 2 0      + 2 4 6      + 4 4 2      +   1 3
```

Subtract.

```
  4 0 0        8 0 0        6 0 0        3 0 0
- 3 0 0      - 1 0 0      - 4 0 0      - 2 0 0
```

```
  8 4 6        7 6 8        3 4 6        5 8 5
- 3 2 1      - 6 1 6      -   3 2      - 2 6 1
```

Perfect score: 20   My score: _____

Lesson 1   Numbers 100 Through 199

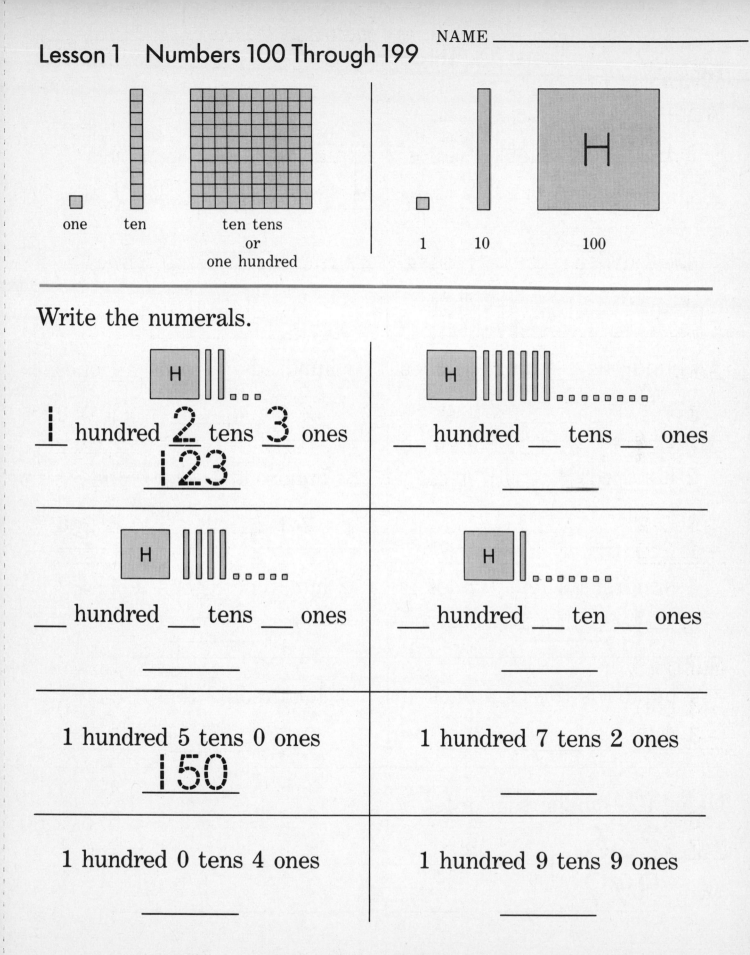

one   ten   ten tens
                or
                one hundred

1   10   100

Write the numerals.

1 hundred 2 tens 3 ones
123

___ hundred ___ tens ___ ones
_____

___ hundred ___ tens ___ ones
_____

___ hundred ___ ten ___ ones
_____

1 hundred 5 tens 0 ones
150

1 hundred 7 tens 2 ones
_____

1 hundred 0 tens 4 ones
_____

1 hundred 9 tens 9 ones
_____

Perfect score: 20   My score: _____

Lesson 2　Numbers 200 Through 499
Write the numerals.

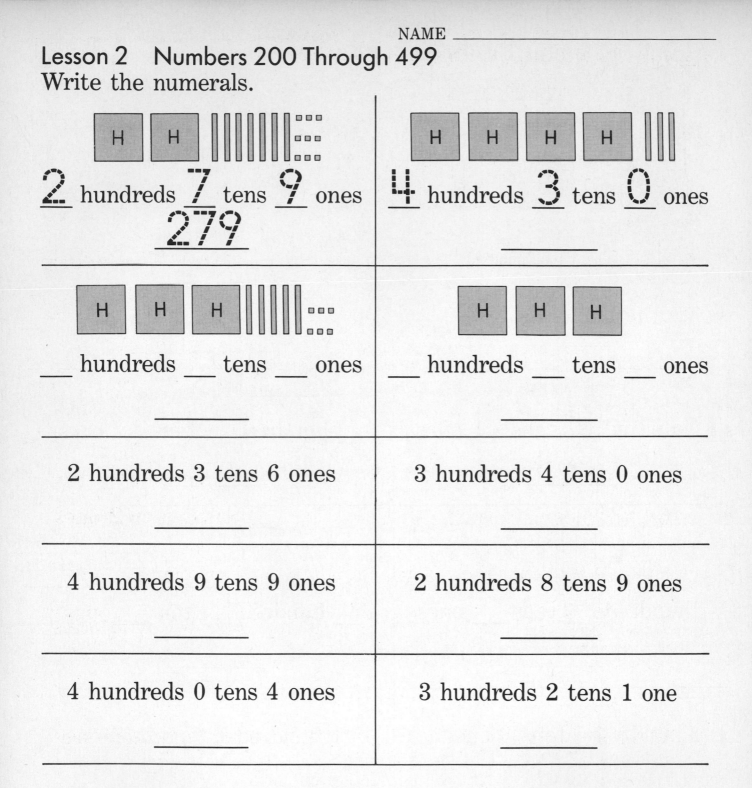

2 hundreds 7 tens 9 ones

279

4 hundreds 3 tens 0 ones

_____

___ hundreds ___ tens ___ ones

_____

___ hundreds ___ tens ___ ones

_____

2 hundreds 3 tens 6 ones

_____

3 hundreds 4 tens 0 ones

_____

4 hundreds 9 tens 9 ones

_____

2 hundreds 8 tens 9 ones

_____

4 hundreds 0 tens 4 ones

_____

3 hundreds 2 tens 1 one

_____

Name the numbers in order.

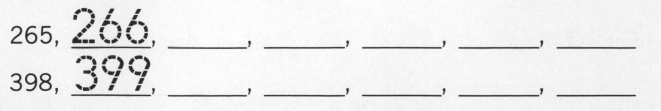

265, 266, _____, _____, _____, _____, _____

398, 399, _____, _____, _____, _____, _____

Perfect score: 34　　My score: _____

92

Lesson 3 Numbers 500 Through 799

Write the numerals.

| H | H | H | H | H | ‖ | H | H | H | H | H | H |

<u>5</u> hundreds <u>2</u> tens <u>0</u> ones   ___ hundreds ___ tens ___ ones

_____   _____

_____

6 hundreds 2 tens 1 one   7 hundreds 1 ten 4 ones

_____   _____

_____

5 hundreds 5 tens 3 ones   6 hundreds 9 tens 7 ones

_____   _____

_____

6 hundreds 7 tens 8 ones   7 hundreds 3 tens 2 ones

_____   _____

_____

7 hundreds 6 tens 5 ones   5 hundreds 8 tens 3 ones

_____   _____

_____

6 hundreds 1 ten 0 ones   7 hundreds 7 tens 6 ones

_____   _____

_____

7 hundreds 9 tens 9 ones   5 hundreds 8 tens 8 ones

_____   _____

Lesson 4   Numbers 800 Through 999
Write the numerals.

__8__ hundreds __2__ tens __5__ ones

_____

___ hundreds ___ ten ___ ones

_____

9 hundreds 2 tens 8 ones

_____

8 hundreds 4 tens 2 ones

_____

8 hundreds 9 tens 2 ones

_____

9 hundreds 0 tens 3 ones

_____

9 hundreds 7 tens 5 ones

_____

8 hundreds 4 tens 0 ones

_____

Count by hundreds to complete the row.

100, _200_, ____, ____, ____, ____, ____, ____, 900

Count by tens to complete the row.

850, 860, ____, ____, ____, ____, ____, ____, ____

Perfect score: 28   My score: _____

94

Lesson 5 Numbers 100 Through 999

Write the numerals.

8 hundreds 6 tens 4 ones _____	5 hundreds 3 tens 8 ones _____
3 hundreds 1 ten 5 ones _____	9 hundreds 8 tens 3 ones _____
1 hundred 0 tens 1 one _____	4 hundreds 2 tens 7 ones _____

Start at 780.
Connect the dots in order.

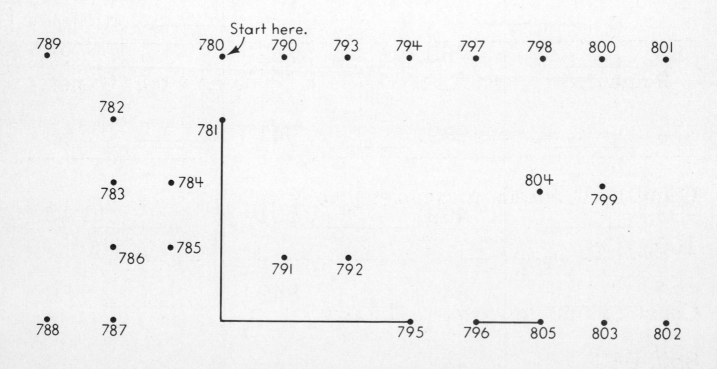

Perfect score: 7   My score: _____

Numbers 100 Through 999

Complete.

After	Between	Before
419, __420__	818, __819__, 820	__770__, 771
301, _____	324, _____, 326	_____, 346
143, _____	606, _____, 608	_____, 160
854, _____	255, _____, 257	_____, 200
209, _____	172, _____, 174	_____, 423
688, _____	760, _____, 762	_____, 950
579, _____	939, _____, 941	_____, 667
993, _____	499, _____, 501	_____, 181
629, _____	847, _____, 849	_____, 800
799, _____	583, _____, 585	_____, 595

Perfect score: 30   My score: _____

NAME _____

5 hundreds	5 0 0	4 hundreds	4 0 0
+3 hundreds	+3 0 0	+5 hundreds	+5 0 0
8 hundreds	8 0 0	9 hundreds	900

Add.

3 hundreds	3 0 0	6 hundreds	6 0 0
+1 hundred	+1 0 0	+2 hundreds	+2 0 0
4 hundreds	400	hundreds	

| 2 0 0 | 1 0 0 | 6 0 0 | 4 0 0 |
| +2 0 0 | +7 0 0 | +3 0 0 | +5 0 0 |

| 3 0 0 | 8 0 0 | 4 0 0 | 7 0 0 |
| +4 0 0 | +1 0 0 | +4 0 0 | +2 0 0 |

| 5 0 0 | 1 0 0 | 5 0 0 | 3 0 0 |
| +1 0 0 | +6 0 0 | +2 0 0 | +2 0 0 |

| 3 0 0 | 4 0 0 | 3 0 0 | 2 0 0 |
| +3 0 0 | +2 0 0 | +5 0 0 | +1 0 0 |

Perfect score: 20   My score: _____

Solve each problem.

Ria packed 300 boxes.

Melvin packed 200 boxes.

How many boxes did Ria and Melvin pack?

$$\begin{array}{r} 300 \\ +200 \\ \hline 500 \end{array}$$

Santo typed 500 letters.

Hale typed 400 letters.

How many letters did they type?

Paula used 100 paper clips.

Milton used 600 paper clips.

How many paper clips did they use?

The grocery store sold 400 red apples.

The grocery store also sold 100 yellow apples.

How many apples did the grocery store sell in all?

Miles worked 200 days.

Julia worked 500 days.

How many days did they work?

Perfect score: 5   My score: _____

NAME _____

```
  2 4 5          ➡      2 4 5          ➡      2 4 5
+ 2 5 3               + 2 5 3               + 2 5 3
──────               ──────               ──────
      8                  9 8              4 9 8
```

Add.

```
  7 4 5                           6 2 3
+   2 3                         + 1 5 6
──────                         ──────
  7 6 8
```

↑ ↑ ↑ — Add the ones.   ↑ ↑ ↑ — Add the ones.
         — Add the tens.   — Add the tens.
         — Add the hundreds.   — Add the hundreds.

```
  4 1 5        5 6 6        3 7 3        1 6 0
+ 3 4 2      +   3 3      + 2 2 1      + 3 3 4
──────       ──────       ──────       ──────


  8 3 5        6 4 2        2 8 7        7 2 3
+   4 2      + 2 5 1      + 4 1 2      +   4 5
──────       ──────       ──────       ──────


  1 3 3        4 5 4        3 1 4        6 5 4
+ 5 2 2      + 3 2 4      + 6 0 2      + 2 3 5
──────       ──────       ──────       ──────
```

Perfect score: 14   My score: _____

99

Problem Solving

Solve each problem.

Gene collected 342 rocks.

Lester collected 201 rocks.

How many rocks did they collect?

$$\begin{array}{r} 342 \\ +201 \\ \hline 543 \end{array}$$

Tina jumped the rope 403 times.

Henry jumped the rope 426 times.

How many times did they jump?

There are 210 people wearing blue hats.

There are 432 people wearing red hats.

How many hats in all?

Asta used 135 paper plates.

Clyde used 143 paper plates.

How many paper plates did they use in all?

Aunt Mary had 536 dollars.

Uncle Lewis had 423 dollars.

How many dollars did they have in all?

Perfect score: 5   My score: _____

Lesson 8 Addition (3 digit)

Add.

$$\begin{array}{r} 340 \\ +225 \\ \hline 565 \end{array}$$

$$\begin{array}{r} 754 \\ + 32 \\ \hline 786 \end{array}$$

$$\begin{array}{r} 826 \\ + 3 \\ \hline \end{array}$$

$$\begin{array}{r} 632 \\ +322 \\ \hline \end{array}$$

$$\begin{array}{r} 198 \\ +200 \\ \hline \end{array}$$

$$\begin{array}{r} 456 \\ + 31 \\ \hline \end{array}$$

$$\begin{array}{r} 541 \\ +333 \\ \hline \end{array}$$

$$\begin{array}{r} 273 \\ +415 \\ \hline \end{array}$$

$$\begin{array}{r} 900 \\ + 34 \\ \hline \end{array}$$

$$\begin{array}{r} 847 \\ +131 \\ \hline \end{array}$$

$$\begin{array}{r} 721 \\ +176 \\ \hline \end{array}$$

$$\begin{array}{r} 402 \\ +383 \\ \hline \end{array}$$

$$\begin{array}{r} 156 \\ +423 \\ \hline \end{array}$$

$$\begin{array}{r} 644 \\ +251 \\ \hline \end{array}$$

$$\begin{array}{r} 215 \\ +542 \\ \hline \end{array}$$

$$\begin{array}{r} 372 \\ +417 \\ \hline \end{array}$$

$$\begin{array}{r} 518 \\ +351 \\ \hline \end{array}$$

$$\begin{array}{r} 783 \\ + 5 \\ \hline \end{array}$$

$$\begin{array}{r} 684 \\ + 14 \\ \hline \end{array}$$

$$\begin{array}{r} 710 \\ +260 \\ \hline \end{array}$$

Perfect score: 20   My score: _____

Problem Solving

Solve each problem.

There are 236 boys in school.
There are 250 girls in school.
How many boys and girls are
in school?

$$\begin{array}{r} 236 \\ +250 \\ \hline \end{array}$$

Mary saw 131 cars.

Marvin saw 268 trucks.

How many cars and trucks did they
see in all?

Jack has 427 pennies.

Jill has 370 pennies.

How many pennies do they
have in all?

There are 582 red apples.

There are 206 yellow apples.

How many apples are there in all?

Ann found 122 shells.

Pedro found 76 shells.

How many shells did they find?

Perfect score: 5   My score: _____

Lesson 9   Subtracting Hundreds

8 hundreds	8 0 0	6 hundreds	6 0 0
−3 hundreds	−3 0 0	−2 hundreds	−2 0 0
5 hundreds	5 0 0	4 hundreds	400

Subtract.

9 hundreds	9 0 0	3 hundreds	3 0 0
−7 hundreds	−7 0 0	−1 hundred	−1 0 0
2 hundreds	200	hundreds	

7 0 0	5 0 0	9 0 0	8 0 0
−3 0 0	−4 0 0	−4 0 0	−5 0 0

6 0 0	3 0 0	5 0 0	4 0 0
−5 0 0	−2 0 0	−1 0 0	−2 0 0

9 0 0	8 0 0	6 0 0	5 0 0
−1 0 0	−4 0 0	−2 0 0	−3 0 0

4 0 0	7 0 0	8 0 0	9 0 0
−1 0 0	−6 0 0	−2 0 0	−6 0 0

Perfect score: 20   My score: _____

103

Problem Solving

Solve each problem.

There were 400 apples in a box.

Jesse took 100 apples from the box.

How many apples are still in the box?

$$\begin{array}{r} 400 \\ -100 \\ \hline 300 \end{array}$$

Tommy bought 300 golf balls.

He gave Irene 200 golf balls.

How many golf balls does he have left?

The black horse ran 900 feet.

The brown horse ran 700 feet.

How many more feet did the black horse run?

The paint store has 800 gallons of paint.

It sells 300 gallons of paint.

How many gallons of paint are left?

There are 700 children.

There are 200 boys.

How many girls are there?

Perfect score: 5   My score: _____

104

Lesson 10   Subtraction (3 digit)

Subtract the ones.

```
  7 4 6
- 4 2 4
------
      2
```

➡ Subtract the tens.

```
  7 4 6
- 4 2 4
------
    2 2
```

➡ Subtract the hundreds.

```
  7 4 6
- 4 2 4
------
  3 2 2
```

Subtract.

```
  8 7 9
-   4 6
------
  8 3 3
```

— Subtract the ones.
— Subtract the tens.
— Subtract the hundreds.

```
  5 8 6
- 1 4 2
------
```

— Subtract the ones.
— Subtract the tens.
— Subtract the hundreds.

```
  6 3 5
- 4 2 3
------
```

```
  4 7 8
- 2 4 1
------
```

```
  3 3 8
-   2 7
------
```

```
  9 5 7
- 7 3 4
------
```

```
  2 9 7
- 1 4 5
------
```

```
  8 4 6
- 3 2 5
------
```

```
  7 6 9
- 5 1 4
------
```

```
  6 5 3
- 1 4 2
------
```

```
  5 6 9
- 3 3 3
------
```

```
  3 6 5
- 2 1 3
------
```

```
  8 1 8
- 6 1 8
------
```

```
  9 3 6
- 4 2 4
------
```

Perfect score: 14   My score: _____

105

Problem Solving

Solve each problem.

The grocery store buys 568 cans of beans.

It sells 345 cans of beans.

How many cans of beans are left?

$$\begin{array}{r} 568 \\ -345 \\ \hline 223 \end{array}$$

The cooler holds 732 gallons of milk.

It has 412 gallons of milk in it.

How many more gallons of milk will it take to fill the cooler?

Ann does 635 push-ups.

Carl does 421 push-ups.

How many more push-ups does Ann do?

Kurt has 386 pennies.

Neal has 32 pennies.

How many more pennies does Kurt have?

It takes 874 nails to build a tree house.

Jillian has 532 nails.

How many more nails does she need?

NAME _____

Subtract.

```
  8 5 6        4 3 2        5 9 8        7 6 9
- 3 5 2      -   2 1      - 4 1 6      - 3 4 5
  5 0 4        4 1 1
```

```
  3 1 9        9 5 4        2 7 5        6 4 3
-     6      - 7 3 1      -     3      - 3 1 3
```

```
  7 7 5        8 3 4        9 4 2        4 7 8
- 2 6 1      -   1 2      - 1 1 1      - 3 2 4
```

```
  5 6 2        4 4 4        3 8 5        7 5 4
- 4 3 1      - 2 1 2      - 1 5 2      -     3
```

```
  8 6 8        9 4 3        6 8 9        5 7 7
- 2 3 4      - 8 4 3      - 4 1 7      -   3 7
```

Perfect score: 20   My score: _____

Problem Solving

Solve each problem.

There were 787 bales of hay.

Glenda fed the cows 535 bales.

How many bales of hay are left?

$$
\begin{array}{r}
787 \\
-535 \\
\hline
252
\end{array}
$$

There are 673 bolts in a box.

Maria took 341 bolts out of the box.

How many bolts are left in the box?

The secretary typed 459 letters.

138 of the letters were mailed.

How many letters are left?

Mr. Jones had 569 dollars

He spent 203 dollars.

How many dollars does he have left?

There are 342 riding horses in the rodeo.

There are 132 bucking horses in the rodeo.

How many more riding horses are there?

Perfect score: 5   My score: _____

Chapter 7   Checkup

Write the numerals.

1 hundred 0 tens 5 ones	9 hundreds 6 tens 4 ones
_____	_____
6 hundreds 1 ten 8 ones	3 hundreds 2 tens 7 ones
_____	_____
3 hundreds 7 tens 1 one	7 hundreds 1 ten 9 ones
_____	_____

Name the numbers in order.

497, 498, _____, _____, _____

Count by tens. Complete the row.

460, _____, _____, _____, 500

Add.

$$\begin{array}{r} 3\;0\;0 \\ +\,5\;0\;0 \\ \hline \end{array} \qquad \begin{array}{r} 4\;0\;0 \\ +\,4\;0\;0 \\ \hline \end{array} \qquad \begin{array}{r} 4\;9\;7 \\ +\,1\;0\;0 \\ \hline \end{array} \qquad \begin{array}{r} 2\;0\;3 \\ +\;\;4\;6 \\ \hline \end{array}$$

Continued on the next page.

Add.

```
  1 2 4        5 2 0        7 3 9        8 6 1
+ 3 2 3      + 4 0 7      + 1 5 0      +   6
```

Subtract.

```
  9 0 0        8 0 0        9 7 4        5 0 8
- 6 0 0      - 2 0 0      - 5 6 4      -   7
```

```
  7 2 8        6 5 7        8 9 4        5 9 6
- 3 2 6      -   4 5      - 4 6 4      - 3 5 2
```

Solve each problem.

There are 275 nails in a box.

123 nails are taken out of the box.

How many nails are still in the box?

_____

Gerald peeled 212 apples.

Anna peeled 84 apples.

How many apples did they peel in all?

Perfect score: 30   My score: _____

Checkup—Chapters 1–4

Complete.

4 tens   6 ones = _____

8 tens   0 ones = _____

Name the next three numbers.

26, 27, 28, _____, _____, _____

91, 92, 93, _____, _____, _____

Count by 10.

10, 20, 30, _____, _____, _____, _____

Add.

7	5	3	8	0
+2	+0	+4	+2	+3

8	9	4	2	9
+4	+9	+7	+9	+7

5	8	7	6	7
+8	+9	+8	+6	+7

Continued on the next page.

Subtract.

9 −6	4 −2	8 −5	6 −1	7 −5
1 0 − 2	1 5 − 7	1 3 − 5	1 1 − 6	1 7 − 8
1 2 − 7	1 8 − 9	1 3 − 9	1 5 − 6	1 6 − 8

How long is each object?

Use a centimeter ruler.

_____ centimeters

Use an inch ruler.

_____ inches

Ring the fraction that tells how much is blue.

$\frac{1}{2}$　　$\frac{1}{3}$　　$\frac{1}{4}$　　　　$\frac{1}{2}$　　$\frac{1}{3}$　　$\frac{1}{4}$　　　　$\frac{1}{2}$　　$\frac{1}{3}$　　$\frac{1}{4}$

Write the time for each clock.

_____ : _____　　　　6:00　　_____ : _____　　　　_____ : _____

Perfect score: 50　　My score: _____

112

FINAL CHECKUP

Add.

8	3	9	8	6	8
+2	+4	+6	+8	+7	+9

			3	10	12
30	41	93	2	20	24
+50	+28	+ 4	+3	+30	+51

38	25	47	200	774	291
+46	+28	+44	+500	+123	+408

Subtract.

9	7	10	12	17	15
−6	−3	− 5	− 3	− 9	− 8

60	39	82	56	96	47
−10	−21	−72	−40	−15	−31

87	50	72	175	384	875
−38	−22	−58	− 62	−270	−641

Continued on the next page.

Complete.

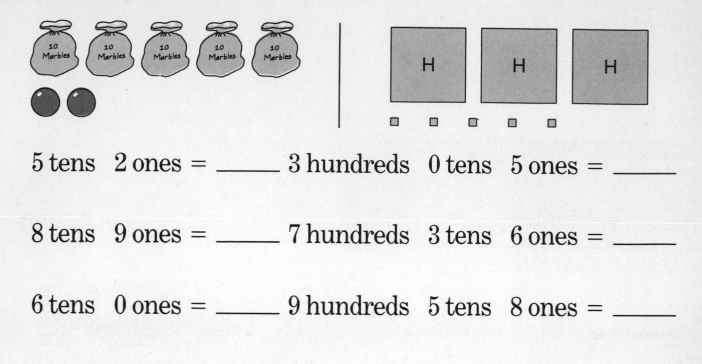

5 tens 2 ones = _____   3 hundreds 0 tens 5 ones = _____

8 tens 9 ones = _____   7 hundreds 3 tens 6 ones = _____

6 tens 0 ones = _____   9 hundreds 5 tens 8 ones = _____

Name the next three numbers.

47, 48, 49, _____, _____, _____

293, 294, 295, _____, _____, _____

Count by 10.

40, 50, 60, _____, _____, _____

500, 510, 520, _____, _____, _____

Continued on the next page.

NAME _____

How long is each object?
Use a centimeter ruler.

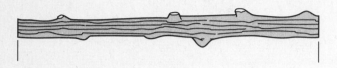

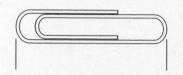

_____ centimeters

_____ centimeters

Use an inch ruler.

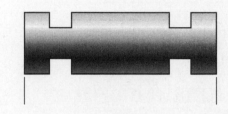

_____ inch

_____ inches

Ring the fraction that tells how much is blue.

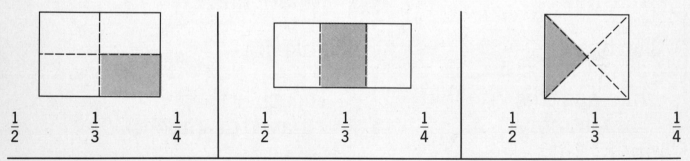

$\frac{1}{2}$ $\frac{1}{3}$ $\frac{1}{4}$ $\frac{1}{2}$ $\frac{1}{3}$ $\frac{1}{4}$ $\frac{1}{2}$ $\frac{1}{3}$ $\frac{1}{4}$

Write the time for each clock.

_____ : _____

_____ : _____

_____ : _____

Continued on the next page.

115

Rinata has	Tao has	Cindy has	Mike has
25¢	30¢	22¢	34¢

Solve each problem.

Rinata has	25¢	Mike has	34¢
Cindy has	−22¢	Tao has	+30¢
Rinata has this much more.	3¢	Together they have this much.	64¢

Mike has	¢	Rinata has	¢
Tao has	− ¢	Mike has	+ ¢
Mike has this much more.	¢	Together they have this much.	¢

Mike has	¢	Cindy has	¢
Rinata has	− ¢	Tao has	+ ¢
Mike has this much more.	¢	Together they have this much.	¢

Perfect score: 70   My score: _____

116

Answers
Math - Grade 2
(Answers for Pre-Tests and Checkups are given on page 123.)

Page 1

3
5
2
       1
       0
       6
    8
    10
    9
    7
    4
0 1 2 3 4 5
  6 7 8 9 10

Page 2

2   1   3   3 2 1

| 4 | 4 | 4 | 4 | 4 |
| 3 | 1 | 2 | 4 | 0 |

| 5 | 5 | 5 | 5 | 5 | 5 |
| 3 | 2 | 4 | 1 | 5 | 0 |

Page 3

6   6   5   1

| 6 | 3 | 6 | 6 | 4 | 2 |

| 7 | 7 | 7 | 7 | 7 | 7 |
| 4 | 3 | 5 | 2 | 6 | 1 |

6 7 6 0 3 4

Page 4

8 8   5   3

| 8 | 8 | 8 | 8 | 8 |
| 4 | 6 | 2 | 7 | 1 |

| 8 | 7 | 6 | 8 | 8 | 8 |
| 7 | 1 | 3 | 3 | 8 | 6 |

Page 5

9   9   5   4

| 9 | 9 | 9 | 9 | 9 | 9 |
| 6 | 3 | 7 | 2 | 8 | 1 |

| 9 | 9 | 7 | 9 | 9 | 8 |
| 4 | 4 | 1 | 6 | 0 | 9 |

Page 6

| 10 | 10 | 10 | 10 | 10 |
| 5 | 6 | 4 | 7 | 3 |

| 10 | 10 | 10 | 10 |
| 8 | 2 | 9 | 1 |

10 10 10 2 7 10

Page 7

9	7	3	8	10	8
6	5	9	10	10	4
9	7	7	10	9	8
4	6	2	1	1	5
6	8	5	2	1	0
6	3	1	7	3	3

Page 8

4	6	4	5	6
+3	−3	+4	−2	+3
7	3	8	3	9

Page 11

1 ten 1 one = 11
1 ten 2 ones = 12
1 ten 3 ones = 13
1 ten 4 ones = 14
1 ten 5 ones = 15
1 ten 6 ones = 16
1 ten 7 ones = 17
1 ten 8 ones = 18

Page 12

2		20		2	5	25
1	9	19		2	8	28
3		30		3	2	32
2	6	26		3	8	38

Page 13

4		40		4	2	42
5	6	56		6	5	65
7		70		7	9	79
8	7	87		9	3	93

Page 14

4	5	45		4	3	43
5		50		5	8	58
6	6	66		7	2	72
8		80		9	9	99

Page 15

46		21	
12		57	
37	78	19	41
24	11	88	34
90	84	67	66
60	35	72	89
53	49	95	20
	96		50

Page 16

0	1	2	3	4	5	6	7	8	9
10	11	12	13	14	15	16	17	18	19
20	21	22	23	24	25	26	27	28	29
30	31	32	33	34	35	36	37	38	39
40	41	42	43	44	45	46	47	48	49
50	51	52	53	54	55	56	57	58	59

Page 17

9	10	11	12
25	26	27	28
40	41	42	43
18	19	20	21
54	55	56	57
47	48	49	50
79	80	81	82
85	86	87	88
71	72	73	74
89	90	91	92
58	59	60	61
96	97	98	99

Page 18

10	20	30	40	50
60	70	80	90	
5	10	15	20	25
30	35	40	45	50
55	60	65	70	75

Page 21

11	11		11	11
11	11		11	11
12	12		12	12
12	12		12	
11	12	12	11	11	11
12	12	12	11	11	12

Page 22

6	8	6	8	9
+5	+4	+6	+3	+3
11	12	12	11	12

Page 23

2	9		3	8
5	6		4	7
4	8		5	7
3	9		6	
8	5	9	3	5	3
4	8	7	6	9	4

Page 24

11	12	11	12	11
−4	−4	−5	−7	−9
7	8	6	5	2

Page 25

13	13		13	13
13	13		14	14
14	14		14	
14	13	13	14	13	14
13	14	14	12	13	13

117

Page 26

8	5
6	9
7	9

5	8	9	5	3	9
8	4	8	4	7	6
5	4	6	9	7	5

Page 27

15	15	15	15
16	16	17	17
16		18	

15	15	18	16	17	15
17	16	16	15	14	14
12	13	13	14	13	12

Page 28

$$\begin{array}{ccccc} 9 & 9 & 7 & 6 & 9 \\ +9 & +7 & +8 & +8 & +8 \\ \hline 18 & 16 & 15 & 14 & 17 \end{array}$$

Page 29

8	7
9	9

9	8	8	8	8	4
9	6	9	7	9	8
7	7	7	5	8	9
9	6	9	4	5	8

Page 30

$$\begin{array}{ccccc} 12 & 10 & 16 & 14 & 18 \\ -3 & -3 & -8 & -9 & -9 \\ \hline 9 & 7 & 8 & 5 & 9 \end{array}$$

Page 31

16	14	15	13	18	14
15	14	14	16	17	13
16	14	15	13	17	15
7	2	8	6	6	9
4	5	6	4	9	5
7	8	6	7	9	5

Page 32

$$\begin{array}{ccccc} 18 & 14 & 10 & 13 & 7 \\ -9 & -6 & +7 & -4 & +9 \\ \hline 9 & 8 & 17 & 9 & 16 \end{array}$$

Page 33

| $\begin{array}{c}9\\-7\\\hline 2\end{array}$ | $\begin{array}{c}3\\+4\\\hline 7\end{array}$ | $\left(\begin{array}{c}12\\-8\\\hline 4\end{array}\right)$ | $5 + 5 = \underline{10}$ | $\begin{array}{c}15\\-8\\\hline 7\end{array}$ | $\begin{array}{c}7\\+5\\\hline 12\end{array}$ | $\begin{array}{c}14\\-9\\\hline 5\end{array}$ |

$11 - 7 = \underline{4}$

| 14 | 5 | 9 | $7 - 6 = \underline{1}$ | $\begin{array}{c}8\\+6\\\hline 14\end{array}$ | $\begin{array}{c}6\\-5\\\hline 1\end{array}$ |

$\begin{array}{c}11\\-3\\\hline 8\end{array}\;9$ $4 + 8 = \underline{12}$

$\begin{array}{c}13\\-8\\\hline 5\end{array}$

$\begin{array}{c}5\\+9\\\hline 14\end{array}$ $\begin{array}{c}9\\+7\\\hline 14\end{array}$ $\begin{array}{c}9\\+5\\\hline 14\end{array}$ $\begin{array}{c}6\\+8\\\hline 14\end{array}$

| $\begin{array}{c}5\\+6\\\hline 11\end{array}$ | $\begin{array}{c}10\\-7\\\hline 3\end{array}$ | $\begin{array}{c}6\\+6\\\hline 12\end{array}$ | $\begin{array}{c}8\\+9\\\hline 17\end{array}$ | $\begin{array}{c}11\\-5\\\hline 6\end{array}$ | $\begin{array}{c}9\\+7\\\hline 16\end{array}$ | $\begin{array}{c}8\\+8\\\hline 16\end{array}$ |

Page 34

$$\begin{array}{ccccc} 17 & 9 & 18 & 8 & 16 \\ -8 & +7 & -9 & +7 & -8 \\ \hline 9 & 16 & 9 & 15 & 8 \end{array}$$

Page 37

1 2 $\frac{1}{2}$	1 2 $\frac{1}{2}$
1 2 $\frac{1}{2}$	1 2 $\frac{1}{2}$
$\frac{1}{2}$	$\frac{1}{2}$

Page 38

1 3 $\frac{1}{3}$	1 3 $\frac{1}{3}$
1 3 $\frac{1}{3}$	1 3 $\frac{1}{3}$
$\frac{1}{3}$	$\frac{1}{3}$

Page 39

1 4 $\frac{1}{4}$	1 4 $\frac{1}{4}$
1 4 $\frac{1}{4}$	1 4 $\frac{1}{4}$
$\frac{1}{4}$	$\frac{1}{4}$

Page 40

$\frac{1}{2}$ $\frac{1}{3}$ $\left(\frac{1}{4}\right)$	$\left(\frac{1}{2}\right)$ $\frac{1}{3}$ $\frac{1}{4}$	$\frac{1}{2}$ $\left(\frac{1}{3}\right)$ $\frac{1}{4}$
$\frac{1}{2}$ $\left(\frac{1}{3}\right)$ $\frac{1}{4}$	$\frac{1}{2}$ $\frac{1}{3}$ $\left(\frac{1}{4}\right)$	$\left(\frac{1}{2}\right)$ $\frac{1}{3}$ $\frac{1}{4}$
$\frac{1}{2}$ $\frac{1}{3}$ $\left(\frac{1}{4}\right)$	$\frac{1}{2}$ $\left(\frac{1}{3}\right)$ $\frac{1}{4}$	$\left(\frac{1}{2}\right)$ $\frac{1}{3}$ $\frac{1}{4}$
$\frac{1}{2}$ $\left(\frac{1}{3}\right)$ $\frac{1}{4}$	$\frac{1}{2}$ $\frac{1}{3}$ $\left(\frac{1}{4}\right)$	$\left(\frac{1}{2}\right)$ $\frac{1}{3}$ $\frac{1}{4}$

Page 41

4 o'clock 4:00	1 o'clock 1:00	12 o'clock 12:00
9 o'clock 9:00	3 o'clock 3:00	11 o'clock 11:00
6 o'clock 6:00	10 o'clock 10:00	7 o'clock 7:00

Page 42

half past 3 3:30	half past 4 4:30	half past 5 5:30
half past 10 10:30	half past 4 4:30	half past 7 7:30
half past 6 6:30	half past 12 12:30	half past 9 9:30

Page 43

7:00

2:00

12:30

Page 44

3
12
3 o'clock

8
12
8 o'clock

12
4
4 o'clock

10
12
10 o'clock

6
1 2
1:30

Page 45

31   4   7   14   5   Thursday

Page 46

12   4   7   February   3   4

Page 47

2		5
	10	
4		7

Page 48

5	1
7	4
11	10
8	13

Page 49

1	2
4	3
	6

Page 50

2		7
	4	
2		1
		3
5		
4		

118

Page 53

17	12	16	12	18	12
13	15	14	14	13	10
13	15	10	10	12	11
9	2	5	8	6	5
4	5	8	8	7	1
7	5	8	8	4	9

Page 54

5 + 6	9 + 2	7 + 9	9 + 7
4 + 7	8 + 3	8 + 8	

8 + 7	6 + 9	8 + 5	7 + 6
7 + 8	9 + 6	9 + 4	6 + 7

15 − 8	13 − 6	17 − 9	15 − 7
14 − 7	16 − 9	12 − 4	13 − 5
		11 − 3	

13 − 7	14 − 8	16 − 7	13 − 4
12 − 6			18 − 9

Page 55

6 tens 60   8 tens 80

40	60	60	70	80
50	70	70	80	20
30	80	90	90	80
90	50	40	90	60

Page 56

20	10	30	40	60
+30	+20	+50	+20	+30
50	30	80	60	90

Page 57

37		57	93	73
95	57	58	95	69
95	69	84	86	97
98	76	89	89	64
81	92	74	77	80

Page 58

25	14	21	31	41
+34	+12	+28	+24	+37
59	26	49	55	78

Page 59

77	76	50	44	78
65	59	94	85	78
77	86	97	98	95
79	37	66	99	96
59	49	55	48	78
96	98	65	22	49

Page 60

Rod
Pam

Rod	Pam
25¢ +20¢ = 45¢	20¢ +32¢ = 52¢
26¢ +20¢ = 46¢	32¢ +26¢ = 58¢
25¢ +32¢ = 57¢	20¢ +25¢ = 45¢

Page 61

2 tens 20   2 tens 20

20	40	10	40	0
40	60	40	10	10
30	30	50	70	20
10	10	30	20	30

Page 62

70	20	60	80	40
−30	−10	−30	−50	−30
40	10	30	30	10

Page 63

73		30	41	30
64	16	93	41	14
47	25	43	60	13
12	10	27	42	57
18	32	82	43	62

Page 64

65¢ −42¢ = 23¢	45¢ −42¢ = 3¢
42¢ −32¢ = 10¢	65¢ −32¢ = 33¢
65¢ −45¢ = 20¢	45¢ −32¢ = 13¢

Page 65

8	8	8	9	9	9
50	60	60	50	80	
58	35	99	67	67	
77	94	87	89	85	

Page 66

35	86		88	7	68
I	T		W	A	S
86	58	58	9	7	59
T	O	O	F	A	R
86	58	88	7	47	39
T	O	W	A	L	K

Page 67

50¢ +25¢ = 75¢	50¢ +30¢ = 80¢
25¢ +20¢ = 45¢	50¢ +40¢ = 90¢
50¢ 25¢ +10¢ = 85¢	50¢ 25¢ +20¢ = 95¢

Page 68

30¢ +34¢ = 64¢	50¢ −30¢ = 20¢
34¢ +25¢ = 59¢	89¢ −25¢ = 64¢
30¢ +25¢ = 55¢	97¢ −34¢ = 63¢

Page 69

67	87	39	70	78	99
48	67	70	98	79	75
35	86	59	97	87	60
81	33	44	50	10	10
16	25	44	22	10	23

Page 70

24	60	55	44	14
+43	−40	−24	+53	23
67	20	31	97	+32
				69

Page 73

13	14	17	13	12	11
15	13	11	18	15	16
70	50	68	75	85	98
9	6	9	5	2	9
9	8	8	7	7	7
10	50	62	32	53	10

Page 74

12	11	14	12	12	13
16	13	12	14	15	11
60	80	95	97	98	57
8	9	9	6	8	8
8	5	7	8	3	3
20	20	35	53	52	23

Page 75

73	32	83	87	93
61	55	64	91	95
91	85	82	74	92

Page 76

51	73	82	92	65
77	85	86	91	63
83	62	91	84	74
92	83	41	82	85
81	82	92	62	75

Page 106

568	732	635	386	874
−345	−412	−421	−32	−532
223	320	214	354	342

Page 107

504	411	182	424
313	223	272	330
514	822	831	154
131	232	233	751
634	100	272	540

Page 108

787	673	459	569	342
−535	−341	−138	−203	−132
252	332	321	366	210

121

Page 9

6	10	9	8	5	4
7	6	10	6	10	3
4	7	9	7	9	10
0	3	4	7	4	5
8	1	1	2	3	2
3	1	3	2	1	4

Page 10

15		23		19
13			20	
34			46	
80			79	
9	10	11	12	
27	28	29	30	
53	54	55	56	
70	71	72	73	

Page 19

28		50	
31		45	
70		82	
66		98	
90		79	
7	8	9	10
40	41	42	43
56	57	58	59
64	65	66	67
81	82	83	84
89	90	91	92

Page 20

7	9	10	9	10	8
12	11	13	12	13	11
14	15	15	13	16	14
3	1	2	6	3	7
4	7	6	8	9	3
9	8	9	7	9	9

Page 35

13	13	14	17	11	14
13	18	15	16	16	15
5	8	3	4	8	5
9	9	8	9	3	7

9	14
+6	−8
15	6

Page 36

$\frac{1}{4}$	$\frac{1}{3}$	$\frac{1}{2}$
4 o'clock	half past 9	8 o'clock
4	7	
3	2	

Page 51

4		7
$\frac{1}{3}$	$\frac{1}{2}$	$\frac{1}{4}$
3		2
10:00	5:30	1:30

Page 52

50	70	90	80	50
78	75	82	97	96
7	6	60	70	90
30	40	30	10	30
61	53	66	51	33

Page 71

68	97	70	99	96	88
8	69	95	87	97	78
12	51	33	70	31	30
11	24	15	46	41	51

53¢	68¢
+32¢	−44¢
85¢	24¢

Page 72

42	33	41	55	92
70	91	91	60	82
41	61	44	51	80
24	6	17	9	19
49	37	17	24	4
13	19	16	28	16

Page 89

42	83	75	81	57
62	92	82	92	31
26	29	19	24	18
45	9	7	34	17

26	26
−18	+36
8	62

Page 90

532	841
486	378

400	900	500	700
689	678	657	639
100	700	200	100
525	152	314	324

Page 109

105	964		
618	327		
371	719		
499, 500, 501			
470, 480, 490, 500			
800	800	597	249

Page 110

447	927	889	867
300	600	410	501
402	612	430	244

275	212
−123	+84
152	296

Page 111

46	80			
29	30	31		
94	95	96		
40	50	60	70	
9	5	7	10	3
12	18	11	11	16
13	17	15	12	14

Page 112

3	2	3	5	2
8	8	8	5	9
5	9	4	9	8
10	2			

$\frac{1}{2}$ $\boxed{\frac{1}{3}}$ $\frac{1}{4}$ | $\frac{1}{2}$ $\frac{1}{3}$ $\boxed{\frac{1}{4}}$ | $\boxed{\frac{1}{2}}$ $\frac{1}{3}$ $\frac{1}{4}$

10:00	6:00	3:30

Page 113

10	7	15	16	13	17
80	69	97	8	60	87
84	53	91	700	897	699
3	4	5	9	8	7
50	18	10	16	81	16
49	28	14	113	114	234

Page 114

52	305	
89	736	
60	958	
50	51	52
296	297	298
70	80	90
530	540	550

Page 115

8	4
1	2

$\frac{1}{2}$ $\frac{1}{3}$ $\boxed{\frac{1}{4}}$ | $\frac{1}{2}$ $\boxed{\frac{1}{3}}$ $\frac{1}{4}$ | $\frac{1}{2}$ $\frac{1}{3}$ $\boxed{\frac{1}{4}}$

10:00	9:30	4:30

Page 116

25¢	34¢
−22¢	+30¢
3¢	64¢
34¢	25¢
−30¢	+34¢
4¢	59¢
34¢	22¢
−25¢	+30¢
9¢	52¢

NOTES

NOTES